JANE GREENOFF

CELEBRATION
CROSS STITCH

JANE GREENOFF

CELEBRATION
CROSS STITCH

David & Charles

Dedication

To the memory of Jane Mason who died
on 5th November 1995, aged 35.
She taught me cross stitch and changed my life.

A DAVID & CHARLES BOOK

First published in the UK in 1996
Reprinted 1996
Text and designs Copyright © Jane Greenoff 1996
Photography and layout Copyright © David & Charles 1996

Jane Greenoff has asserted her right to be identified as author of this work
in accordance with the Copyright, Designs and Patents Act, 1988.

A catalogue record for this book is available from the British Library.

ISBN 0 7153 0143 8

Photography by David Johnson
Book design by Kit Johnson
Typeset by Ace Filmsetting Ltd, Frome, Somerset
and printed in Italy by Nuovo Istituto Italiano d'Arti Grafiche – Bergamo
for David & Charles
Brunel House Newton Abbot Devon

CONTENTS

ɪNTRODUCTION

*Often, a first attempt at cross stitch is a direct result of the wish to celebrate a
particular event, to give a special gift – to a bride, a new baby or a dear friend. Many people
find that this first attempt opens the door to the addictive hobby of counted cross stitch.
When I meet groups of stitchers, and particularly these cross stitch addicts, I am often asked for
designs suitable for family celebrations and traditional festivals.
This book is a result of that public demand.*

The designs contained within *Celebration Cross Stitch* are inspired by this idea of giving and receiving gifts, with the projects based around everyday celebrations, traditions and events. In many cases familiar objects have been used as the basic design idea or motif – a clock, a calendar, a teacup, a favourite flower. Most of the designs have been created specifically to be mixed and matched, so practically any occasion can be celebrated.

I hope this book will change the way you think of counted needlework. I have included plenty of traditional counted cross stitch designs, worked on both Aida fabric and some of the wonderful new evenweaves available. I have also added projects with a contemporary flavour. Counted cross stitch is, of course, well represented but there are also some new techniques, including pulled thread, Hardanger embroidery and cutwork. These will not only challenge you and add interest and dimension to your work but will be great fun to stitch.

The book begins with a useful Basic Techniques section, which explains all you need to know about the materials, equipment and techniques used in the projects. After this, the book is divided into three parts.

The Passage of Time features some unusual projects, all inspired by the idea of time passing.

A Celebration of Life has a wealth of more traditional projects for the events that colour our lives – births, christenings, birthdays, weddings, anniversaries, moving home, retirement.

Celebrations Through the Year is the sparkling part of the book providing over twenty projects for special times of the year, such as Valentine's Day, Easter, Bonfire Night and, of course, Christmas.

Each project has been given a skill rating to help you choose the right project for you, particularly if you are a beginner. The skill levels are:

1 Projects using complete cross stitches on Aida fabric – perfect for beginners.
2 Projects using complete and part cross stitches and French knots on Aida.
3 Projects using cross stitch on an evenweave fabric, e.g. linen.
4 Projects using a variety of counted stitches on evenweave fabrics.
5 Projects using composite stitches, pulled and drawn thread and Hardanger embroidery on evenweave fabrics.

Remember, this book is a celebration of a wonderful hobby, not from a trained expert, but from someone who stitches for a living and still loves it! The basic stitching instructions are personal and have been developed over hundreds of hours of designing and stitching. I hope you find them simple to follow and that they increase your enjoyment from this, my eleventh book.

$\mathcal{B}$ASIC TECHNIQUES

It is important to read this section carefully as it contains information necessary for the successful completion of the projects. Aspects of planning and design are described, the materials and equipment required, how to start and finish and descriptions of the techniques and stitches used.
Imperial measurements are given throughout with the approximate metric equivalent in brackets. In all cases I have adjusted the measurements to the nearest ¼ in with the metric equivalent to match.

COUNTED CROSS STITCH

All counted designs are made up of squares or parts of squares. The principle is that the picture, pattern or motif is transferred to the fabric by matching the weave of the fabric to the pattern or chart. The term counted means that the design is transferred on to the fabric by counting the squares on the chart and matching this on the fabric, so that each stitch will be put in the right place.

The designs in this book are worked from large colour charts in counted cross stitch and/or other counted stitches. All the designs may be adapted, mixed and matched, although some of the projects are not suitable for Aida material, requiring an evenweave fabric to achieve the most satisfying results. To reproduce the designs that you see in the colour photographs, you will need to use the fabric recommended at the beginning of each project and DMC stranded cottons (floss) or Perlé thread.

I have included my own DMC/Anchor yarn conversion chart at the back of the book.

THE CHARTS

The needlework charts are illustrated in colour, with or without a symbol, to aid colour identification. Each square, both occupied and unoccupied, represents one block of Aida fabric and two threads of linen, unless otherwise stated. Each occupied square equals one stitch. At this stage each stitch can be presumed to be a complete cross stitch.

All that determines the size of a cross stitch design is the number of stitches up and down and the thread count of the fabric. If you are familiar with knitting, it is similar to the difference in size between the same number of stitches worked in four-ply wool and in a chunky weight wool.

CALCULATING DESIGN SIZE

To calculate the design size, look at the chart and count the number of stitches in each direction. Divide this number by the number of stitches to 1 in (2.5 cm) on the fabric of your choice and this will determine the completed design size. You always need to add a margin for stretching, framing or finishing. I suggest adding 5 in (13 cm) to both dimensions as a rule of thumb, although when working small projects like cards, pincushions and box tops, this rule can be relaxed.

Always check the stitch count and fabric size before starting any of the counted projects in this book, as a slight change of fabric or stitch count may vary the completed design size considerably. It is always important to make sure the design will fit the frame, card or box you intend to use before beginning.

PLANNING LAYOUT CHARTS

This section is included to help you adapt charts to suit a personal occasion. I always use Chartwell graph paper with a light grey grid and a light but not white background. I usually use the imperial version, ie 10 squares to 1 in (2.5 cm) which makes counting squares easier.

It is not necessary to copy all the detail when planning layouts. The coloured charts in this book are drawn with a solid outline, which you may choose not to stitch, but can be copied simply to mark the position of motifs within the overall design.

Decide on the completed size of the stitched project and select the fabric you intend to use. You should at least know the thread count even if you do not have the actual material.

Mark on the graph paper with a soft pencil where the centre and the extremes of the chart should appear. This then becomes the master sheet.

Using a soft pencil, copy the outlines of the motifs you have selected on to another piece of graph paper. When you have copied all the motifs you require, it is quite simple to cut out each section and lay it in position on the master sheet. When you are satisfied with the layout, you can begin stitching using the colour charts from the book.

CHOOSING THE RIGHT FABRIC

The fabrics used for counted cross stitch are all woven so that they have the same number of threads or blocks to 1 in (2.5 cm) in both directions. The warp and weft are woven evenly so that when a stitch is formed it will appear as a square or part of a square.

When choosing fabrics for counted cross stitch, you should remember that the thread count is the method used by manufacturers to differentiate between the varieties available, so the higher the number or the more threads or stitches to 1 in (2.5 cm) the finer the fabric will be.

AIDA

This excellent cotton fabric is woven for counted needlework and is ideal for the beginner. The threads are woven in blocks rather than singly. There are many projects that suit this fabric particularly well as it forms a very pretty square stitch. Aida is available in 8, 11, 14, 16 and 18 blocks to 1 in (2.5 cm). If you require an even finer stitch count, it is possible to use Hardanger fabric at 22 blocks to 1 in (2.5 cm).

Aida is available in a wide variety of solid colours and now in rustic mixtures like Zweigart, Yorkshire and Rustico which can add character to a project.

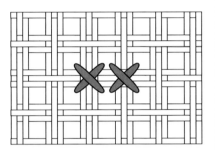

Fig 1 Cross stitch on Aida

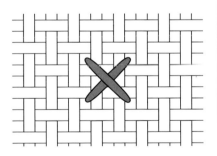

Fig 2 Cross stitch on linen

When stitching on Aida, one block on the fabric corresponds to one square on the chart. Working a cross stitch on Aida is exactly the same as on linen, except that instead of counting threads you count the single blocks (see figs 1 and 2). For working on linen, see next column.

Fig 3 Three quarter stitch worked on linen

Forming three-quarter stitches on Aida is less accurate than on linen, because you need to pierce the centre of the square block.

EVENWEAVES

This is the title given to the range of fabrics where the threads are woven singly rather than in blocks and includes linen, Jobelan, Linda and many others. Where I have indicated the need for an evenweave fabric, any of the following will suit admirably.

LINEN

This lovely, if slightly more expensive material, made from flax, is commonly used for counted cross stitch. Stitching on linen is no more complicated than stitching on Aida, but requires a different technique. Linen has irregularities or slubs in the fabric, which occur naturally and add to the charm of the finished work, and is ideal when you are trying to emulate the style of an antique piece. There are even fabrics available where the manufacturer has added the slubs artificially to copy the effect of linen (see All Things Wild, page 37).

To even out any discrepancies, cross stitches on linen are generally worked over two threads in each direction, although I will explain stitching on linen in more detail later in this section.

Linen is now available in white, antique white, cream, raw or natural shades and in a variety of dyed colours.

JOBELAN

Jobelan is the trade name for a range of specialist needlework materials which includes an excellent evenweave fabric made of cotton and modal (Article 429 and Article 449). It is easy to wash and iron and is an ideal medium for counted needlework as it is woven in single threads rather than blocks (similar to linen) and is available in over forty wonderful colours!

AFGHAN FABRICS

These soft fabrics made from mixed fibres are produced for shawl-like projects which can look wonderful thrown over the back of a chair. They are usually sold in squares or pattern repeats.

STITCHING PAPER

This product is based as closely as possible on the early Victorian punched paper. The original perforated or punched paper was made in England possibly as early as 1840. Early examples of it were bought as small decorated circles or squares and were used to decorate empty spaces in scrap books. The Victorians loved working on the paper and produced bookmarks, needlecases, pincushions, glove and handkerchief boxes, notebook covers and greetings cards.

Stitching Paper is a useful material – it can be stitched, folded, glued and cut to make

pretty cross stitch projects as illustrated in the colour pictures on pages 30, 47, 88, 92 and 106.

TIPS FOR STITCHING ON PAPER

1. Although the paper is quite strong, do remember that it needs to be handled with care.
2. There is a right and a wrong side to the paper, the smoother side being the right side.
3. Avoid folding the paper unless this is part of the design.
4. Find the centre with a ruler and mark with a pencil. Pencil lines can be removed with a soft rubber.
5. Use three strands of embroidery cotton (floss) for the cross stitch and one or two strands for any outlining.
6. Work any outlining in backstitch after the cross stitch is complete.
7. When the stitching is complete, cut out the design using the cutting line on the chart as a guide (if shown) or leaving one complete square around the stitching.

THREADS

For all the projects in this book I have selected DMC stranded cotton (floss) for the cross stitch with the exception of Perlé for the Hardanger embroidery. Stranded cotton (floss) is a six-ply mercerised cotton which is usually divided before stitching. At the beginning of each project I have indicated how many strands of stranded cotton (floss) are used in the example in the colour picture. If you alter the fabric selection for a particular project, remember to check the number of threads needed for that fabric. If you are stitching on linen and you are not

sure of the number of strands needed for the cross stitch, the best way is to carefully pull out a thread of the fabric and compare this with your chosen yarn. The thread on your needle should be roughly the same weight as that of the fabric.

When selecting threads, always have the fabric you are intending to use close at hand, because the colour of your background fabric will affect the choice of colours. When in a shop, check the colour of the thread in daylight as electric light can 'kill' some shades. It is possible to buy daylight simulation bulbs to use in normal spotlights at home – a great help when shading a design in the evening.

It is best to use an organiser for your threads – it really does pay to start with good habits. There are many excellent organiser systems on the market, but I make my own organiser cards as shown in fig 4.

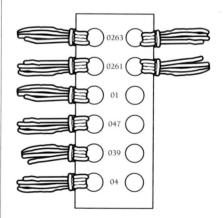

Fig 4 Thread organiser

The card from inside a packet of tights is excellent, but any stiff card will do. Punch holes down each side and, taking a skein of stranded cotton (floss), cut the cotton into manageable lengths of about 31 in (80 cm), double them and thread them through the holes as shown. It is quite simple to remove one length of thread from the card without disturbing the rest. Label the card with the manufacturer's name and shade number.

Stranded cotton (floss) can be used in conjunction with Balger blending filament, which is a gossamer-thin yarn that will add lustre and sparkle to your design.

NEEDLES

With all counted cross stitch you will need blunt tapestry needles of various sizes, depending on which fabric you choose. The most commonly used tapestry needles for cross stitch are sizes 24 and 26, but you may find you need a size 22 when using Perlé for Hardanger embroidery. Avoid leaving your needle in the fabric when it is put away as it may leave a mark. The nickel plating on needles varies so much that some stitchers find that their needles discolour and mark their hands and fabric. As a result, they treat themselves to gold-plated needles which may be used again and again (see Suppliers, page 133).

I have indicated a needle size for each project, but it is simple to select the correct size by pushing the needle through the fabric. It should pass through without enlarging the hole, but also should not fall through without any pressure applied.

When beads are suggested in a project, they may be attached using a fine, sharp needle and a half cross stitch. Beading needles are available but can be expensive if used rarely.

FRAMES AND HOOPS

This subject always raises questions and argument. It is not necessary to use a frame or hoop for cross stitch on evenweave or Aida. Having said that, it is a matter of personal choice and if you prefer to use one, then please do so! If you do use a hoop, ensure that all the design is within the stitching area of the hoop and that you do not need to move the hoop across worked areas, as this may drag and spoil your stitches.

SCISSORS

Keep a small, sharp pair of pointed scissors exclusively for your stitching. To avoid hunting for them down the side of the sofa, wear them around your neck on a piece of ribbon!

A CROSS STITCH

A cross stitch has two parts and can be worked in one of two ways. A complete stitch can be worked, or a number of half stitches may be stitched in one line, then completed on the return journey (see fig 5). I prefer to work my cross stitches in two journeys, using a sewing movement, since this is both quicker and keeps the back neater

Fig. 5 Part completed stitches – completed on return journey

and less padded. The one essential rule is that all the top stitches must face in the same direction.

Stitching Tip: If you work the cross stitches using a sewing movement, the threads have a tendency to twist and turn. If you learn to turn your needle just a fraction as you leave the stitch, the threads stay smooth and untangled (practice makes perfect!)

HOW TO STITCH

For this example the cross stitch is being worked on linen, over two threads of fabric, using two strands of stranded cotton (floss). When working counted stitches on a single-weave fabric like linen or Jobelan, always start the stitching to the left of a vertical thread (see fig 6) which appears as a larger, easier hole to see and acts as a warning if you have miscounted. You should always be in the same position i.e. to the left of a vertical thread, so if you have made a mistake you will see it quickly.

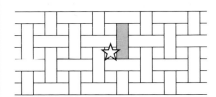

Fig 6 Starting the stitching to the left of a vertical thread

Bring the needle up through the wrong side of the fabric at the bottom left, cross two fabric threads and insert in the top right. Push the needle through, then bring it up at the bottom right-hand corner, ready to complete the stitch in the top left-hand corner. To work the adjacent stitch, bring the needle up at the bottom right-hand corner of the first stitch (thus the stitches share points of entry and exit). To make part-completed stitches, work the first leg of the cross stitch as above, but instead of completing the stitch, work the next half stitch and continue to the end of the row. The cross is completed on the return journey.

WHERE AND HOW TO START

It can be nerve-wracking at the start, when you are faced with a plain unprinted piece of fabric, but it is really very simple. The secret is to start in the middle of the fabric and in the middle of the chart, unless otherwise stated. Using this method, there will always be enough fabric to stretch and frame. To find the middle of the fabric, fold it in four and press lightly. Open out and work a narrow line of tacking (basting) stitches along the fold lines, starting to the left of a vertical thread and following the threads to mark the fold and the centre (see fig 7). These stitches are removed when the work has been completed.

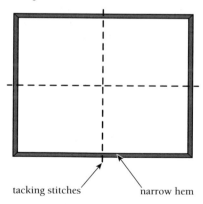

Fig 7 Fold the fabric in four and tack (baste) along the folds

Check that you have all the colours you need and mount all the threads on a piece of card alongside its

shade number. Sew a narrow hem or oversew the raw edges of your fabric to prevent fraying. This can be removed on completion. Thread your needle with the required number of strands and you are ready to go!

Having learnt the basic cross stitch and discovered where you need to start, you now need to know how to start off, using the knotless loop start. This method can be very useful with stranded cotton (floss), but it only works if you are intending to stitch with an *even* number of threads, ie 2, 4 or 6. Cut the stranded cotton (floss) roughly twice the length you would normally need and carefully separate one strand. Double this thread and thread your needle with the two ends. Pierce your fabric from the wrong side where you intend to place your first stitch, leaving the looped end at the rear of the work (see fig 8). Return your needle to the wrong side after forming a half cross stitch, and pass the needle through the waiting loop. The stitch is thus anchored and you may begin to stitch.

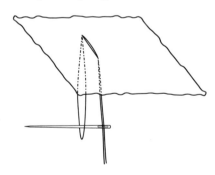

Fig 8 Knotless loop start

When working with an *uneven* number of threads, start by anchoring the thread at the front of the work, away from and above the stitching area. This thread can be stitched into the back of the work when stitches have been formed.

HOW TO FINISH

When a group of stitches or a length of thread is completed, there are two methods of finishing off. At the back of the work, pass the needle under a few stitches of the same or similar colour and snip off the loose end close to the stitching. Small loose ends have a nasty habit of pulling through to the right side! Another method, that also prevents any distortion of the stitches on the right side of the project, is to finish the thread in the same direction as you are stitching. To do this, leave the loose end to one side. Start a new thread, work a few stitches, re-thread the loose end and pass it under the new stitches, thus following the stitching direction.

BACKSTITCH OUTLINING

Outlining is the addition of a backstitch outline to add detail or dimension to the picture. In all the charts in this book the solid lines surrounding the black and white

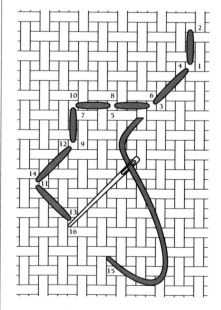

Fig 9 Back stitch outlining

symbols refer to a backstitch outline and include a suggested DMC shade number. Outlining is very much an optional part of cross stitch. You will see as you look through the book that outlining is not always necessary and is often a matter of taste.

WASHING AND PRESSING CROSS STITCH

When a piece of cross stitch is complete, it may be necessary to wash the item before finishing. Washing can give a piece of stitching a new life, but can also ruin your work if care is not taken. Drinks, ice cream and cats cause havoc so always keep your stitching covered and away from all of them.

If it becomes necessary to wash a piece of stitching, DMC and Anchor threads usually prove to be colour-fast. However, some reds can bleed, so always check for colour-fastness before immersing the project completely. To do this, dampen a white tissue and press the red stitches at the back of the work. Remove the tissue and look for any traces of red colour. If any colour is visible on the tissue, avoid washing this project.

If the item is colour-fast, wash it using bleach-free soap and hand-hot water, squeezing gently but never rubbing or wringing. Rinse in plenty of warm water and dry naturally. You should never use a tumble dryer.

To iron cross stitch, heat the iron to a hot setting and use the steam button if your iron has one. Cover the ironing board with a *thick* layer of towelling. Place the stitching on the towelling, right side down with the back of the work facing you. Press the fabric quite firmly and you will see how much this improves the appearance of your stitching. Leave the embroidery to cool and dry completely before framing or making up.

AGEING LINEN

It is easy to add the appearance of age to a piece of linen or lace by dipping it in black tea. It is possible to age a completed piece of needlework by dipping the whole thing in black tea, although you must check that the colours are fast before you attempt this. After dipping the fabric or needlework, allow to dry naturally and press as described above.

TWEEDING

This practice is a simple way to increase the numbers of colours in your palette without buying more thread. To tweed, combine more than one coloured thread in the needle at the same time, and work as one (this technique is particularly effective when working French knots).

HARDANGER EMBROIDERY

Hardanger embroidery originates from the Hardanger region in western Norway. The exact origin of the work is not known, although Norwegian drawn work (later known as Hardanger) thrived in that country as early as the seventeenth century and was used to decorate household linens, aprons and skirts. The decorative element in this type of counted needlework are the holes and cut work patterns.

KLOSTER BLOCKS

Kloster blocks create a framework for the cut areas in Hardanger. They are worked in patterns forming enclosed areas which can then be cut and decorated.

A kloster block is formed by working five vertical or five horizontal straight stitches over four threads on an evenweave fabric or four blocks if working on Hardanger fabric. The stitches are worked side by side following the grain of the fabric, vertically or horizontally. The kloster blocks are worked in groups or diagonal steps where the corners of the blocks share a hole (see fig 10a). Do not let thread cross over open space on the back of the fabric (see fig 10b).

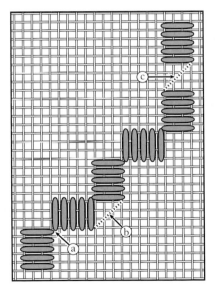

Fig 10 Working kloster blocks

However, when working unconnected groups of kloster blocks you can move to the next group by running the thread at an angle at the back of the fabric (see fig 10c). As you work the blocks, keep checking that the stitches are counted correctly and that the blocks are opposite each other (see fig 11).

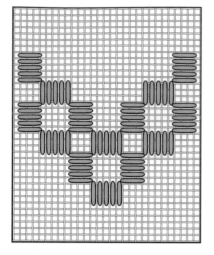

Fig 11 A second row of kloster blocks connects to the first

CUTTING THE THREADS

When the kloster blocks have been stitched, the threads between them are cut and drawn out. This is always the area which causes anxiety. The secret is to work *all* the kloster blocks, checking that you have counted correctly and that the blocks are exactly opposite each other. Then, using very sharp, pointed scissors, cut the threads at the *base* of the kloster block where the straight stitches enter the fabric, *not* at the side at the long edge of the stitch (see fig 12). You will be cutting four threads at the end of each kloster block. Take your time, cutting carefully and counting each thread.

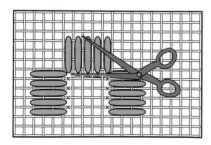

Fig 12 Cutting the threads

When you pull out the cut threads the result should be similar to fig 13 below.

NEEDLEWEAVING

The loose threads remaining within the kloster blocks are woven into covered bars producing an open square which can be filled with a decorative stitch, such as dove's eye (see fig 14). A slightly finer thread is used to work the covered bars and decorative stitches than the kloster blocks. To weave a bar, bring the needle up in the centre of the loose threads and work over and under pairs of threads (see figs 13a–c).

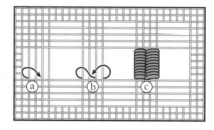

Fig 13 Needleweaving

DOVE'S EYE STITCH

This decorative filling is stitched as you needleweave. On the final side of the square, needleweave half the bar, then work loops through the centre of each bar as shown in fig 14. Needleweave the remaining half of the last bar.

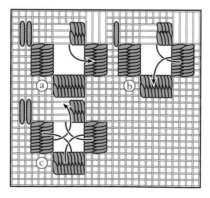

Fig 14 Dove's eye stitch

EYELET STITCH

Where the threads are not cut and drawn within a kloster block, the centre can be decorated with an eyelet stitch (see fig 15).

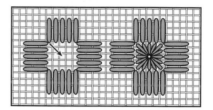

Fig 15 Eyelet stitch

ADDITIONAL STITCHES

All the stitches in this book are used as counted stitches, although some of them are also used in surface embroidery and crewel work. I find that the use of additional stitches can bring a new dimension to a piece of cross stitch.

LAZY DAISY STITCH

This pretty stitch, more usually found in surface embroidery, can be very effective when combined with cross stitch and particularly so when worked in silk ribbon. Keep the thread or silk ribbon untwisted as you form the stitch and do not pull the stitch too tight.

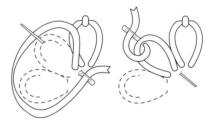

Fig 16 Lazy daisy stitch

FRENCH KNOTS

French knots are useful little stitches and may be used in addition to cross stitch. Bring the needle up to the right side of the fabric, wind the thread around the needle twice and post the needle through to the back, one thread or part of a block away from the entry point. This stops the stitch pulling to the wrong side. Before pulling the needle through to the wrong side, tighten the threads on the needle slightly to make a neat knot. If you want bigger knots, add more thread to the needle as this seems to give a better finish than winding more times. Random uncounted French knots are almost free embroidery without the panic and are great fun. I outline the area with a single line of backstitch and then pack in the French knots until the area is completely covered (see Time to Stitch, page 19).

Fig 17 Working a French knot

DOUBLE CROSS STITCH

The double cross stitch in this book has been worked over four threads. Work a cross stitch first, then add a vertical cross on top. Keep the direction of the stitch uniform.

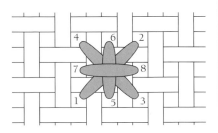

Fig 18 Double cross stitch

LONG-LEGGED CROSS STITCH

This stitch covers two threads of linen vertically and four horizontally and is worked from left to right, forming an attractive braided effect.

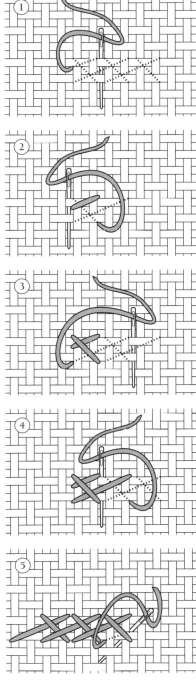

Fig 19 Working a long-legged cross stitch – stages 1–5

ALGERIAN EYE

This is a pretty star-shaped stitch which may be added to cross stitch with great effect. The stitch occupies the space taken by four cross stitches and is worked in such a way that a small hole is formed. Keep the hole in the centre of the stitch free of loose threads or they will show through.

Fig 20 Algerian eye

SATIN STITCH

This is a long smooth stitch which covers the fabric. You may need to experiment with the number of strands of stranded cotton (floss) needed to achieve the desired padded effect.

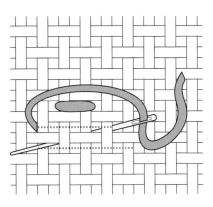

Fig 21 Satin stitch

TIME TO STITCH

*This unusual sampler, decorated with
time-related charms and pieces of old clocks, will
serve to remind you that, no matter how busy
your life may be, you should always make time
for one of life's more relaxing activities –
cross stitch embroidery.*

SKILL LEVEL 2
STITCH COUNT: 185 × 143
DESIGN SIZE: 13½ × 10¼ in (34 × 26 cm)

MATERIALS
18½ × 15½ in (47 × 39.5 cm) beige Aida,
14 blocks to 1 in (2.5 cm)
Stranded cottons (floss) as listed on the chart
Assorted charms and clock pieces
(see Suppliers page 133)

1. Work a narrow hem or zig-zag around the
raw edges to prevent fraying. Fold in four, press
lightly and mark the folds with a line of tacking
(basting) stitches.

2. Following the chart on pages 20 and 21, work
the cross stitch starting at the centre, using two
strands of stranded cotton (floss) for the cross
stitch and one for the backstitch outline. The
thyme flower motifs are worked in random
uncounted French knots in assorted pinks, ecru
and lemon.

3. When the stitching is complete, check
carefully for any missed stitches and then press
lightly on the wrong side.

4. Add the charms at random using one strand
of matching thread and a half cross stitch.

5. Stretch and frame as desired (see page 126).

367

310

THE PERPETUAL ALMANAC

*This interesting idea not only makes an original cross stitch piece but a useful one,
enabling you to discover the day of the week of any date you choose far into the
future. My design is an up-to-date version of one stitched by a schoolgirl in 1787. This
version took my husband hours of research to prove. The project is given an apt
astrological flavour by the inclusion of orbiting planets and stars. It is worked in cross
stitch and backstitch with the addition of small sequins. If you intend to give
this to a friend, it would be kind to include instructions!*

SKILL LEVEL 3
STITCH COUNT: 214 × 258
DESIGN SIZE: 14¼ × 17¼ in (35.5 × 44 cm)
〜
MATERIALS
20 × 23 in (50 × 58.5 cm) slate-grey linen,
30 threads to 1 in (2.5 cm)
Stranded cottons (floss) as listed on the chart
Tapestry needle size 26
Sharp or beading needle
Assorted small sequins and beads (optional)

1. Fold the fabric in four, press lightly and mark
the folds with tacking (basting) stitches. If working
on an evenweave fabric, remember to begin
tacking to the left of a vertical thread (see Where
and How to Start, page 12).

2. Following the charts on pages 26–29, count
from the centre and work the cross stitches using
two strands of stranded cotton (floss). Work the
grid and the numbers in one strand, in the colour
indicated on the chart key.

3. When you have completed the stitching, check
for missed stitches and press lightly on the wrong
side.

4. Using a sharp needle and matching thread, add
the sequins and beads at random. Stretch and
frame as desired (see page 126).

HOW TO USE THE ALMANAC

● Choose a date in the future of which you wish to
know the day of the week. Then from your chosen
date find the year on the left-hand table.
● At the head of that year's column is a dominical
letter – note which one.
● Find the month of your chosen date in the
middle column and, reading to the right, find the
matching dominical letter.
● Listed above this letter are the dates of the
Sundays in that month. From these dates you can
pinpoint the weekday of your chosen date.
● If your chosen date occurs in January or
February of a leap year, follow the first four steps
but go back one day. (On this table the leap years
are preceded by a blank box.)

〜
*Opposite **This fascinating project will prove to
be a talking point with all your friends as it
shows how to find the day of the week of any
day in the future.***

YOU ARE MY SUNSHINE

This lively fun project uses the bright sun motif from The Perpetual Almanac chart and I have added a line of popular music to celebrate a special friendship.

SKILL LEVEL 2
STITCH COUNT: 140 × 101
DESIGN SIZE: 11¼ × 8¼ in (28.5 × 21 cm)

MATERIALS
15½ × 12¼ in (39 × 31 cm) grey linen, 25 threads to 1 in (2.5 cm)

Stranded cottons (floss) as listed on the chart

Tapestry needle size 26

Graph paper and pencil

A purchased frame

1. Fold the fabric in four, press lightly and mark the folds with tacking (basting) stitches. If working on an evenweave fabric, begin tacking to the left of a vertical thread (see Where and How to Start, page 12). Set the fabric aside while you plan the layout of the words and music.

2. Using the graph paper and pencil, count out the area occupied by the words (charted on pages 26–27) and the music (see Planning Layout Charts, page 8). You only need to draw this as a box because you can stitch the design from the chart in the book. Add the outline of the sun motif from The Perpetual Almanac, centre the new chart and you are ready to begin stitching.

3. Work the cross stitch sun motif, text and musical notes using two strands of stranded cotton (floss). Use one strand only to stitch the manuscript lines.

4. When the stitching is complete, check for missed stitches and press lightly on the wrong side. Stretch and frame as desired (see page 126).

SPINNING PLANETS CLOCK

Adapted from The Perpetual Almanac chart, the clock face of this distinctive project is decorated with orbiting planets and stars.

SKILL LEVEL 2
STITCH COUNT: 58 × 71
DESIGN SIZE: 4½ × 5¼ in (11.5 × 13.5 cm)

MATERIALS
8 × 9½ in (20 × 24 cm) Jobelan fabric
(Article 429, shade 61),
28 threads to 1 in (2.5 cm)

Stranded cottons (floss) as listed on the chart

Tapestry needle size 26

Graph paper and pencil

Purchased Perspex clock kit (see Suppliers, page 133)

1. Fold the fabric in four, press lightly and mark the folds with tacking (basting) stitches. If working on an evenweave fabric, begin tacking to the left of a vertical thread (see Where and How to Start, page 12). Set aside while you plan the clock face.

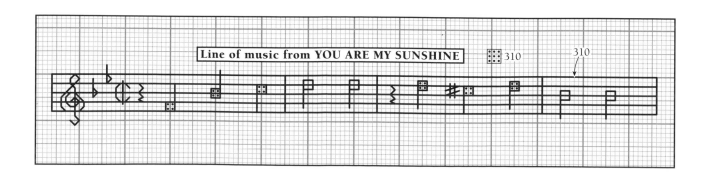

Line of music from YOU ARE MY SUNSHINE   310   310

2. Using the graph paper and pencil, mark a position for the clock spindle and copy the clock numbers from the chart on page 125. Add the outlines of the planets and stars you wish to include from the charts on pages 26–29 and you are ready to stitch.

3. Work the cross stitch and backstitch numerals in two strands of stranded cotton (floss), keeping the top stitch facing in the same direction. Use one strand of the colour indicated to outline the planets if necessary.

This bright, jolly picture has been produced by taking the sunshine motif from the Perpetual Almanac chart and adding the musical notes which play out 'You Are My Sunshine' to help you to celebrate a special friendship.

4. When the stitching is complete, check for missed stitches and make up by following the manufacturer's instructions.

 A CELEBRATION OF LIFE

*This section of the book reflects the events that affect
our lives – births, christenings, birthdays, engagements, weddings,
anniversaries, new homes. There is something for every taste: from the delicately shaded
traditional Pastel Lace Birth Sampler (pictured opposite) to the boldly modern
Congratulations Banner; from the practical 'Well Done' Message Board to the
purely decorative Magnolia Wedding Ring Pillow. Several of the designs
use exciting techniques such as cutwork and Hardanger embroidery for those of
you looking for something a little different.*

~

*A single red rose is a symbol of love, so for a special occasion, the Wild Rose
Trinket Pot and Card set in soft pink will make romantic gifts
to be treasured by those you love.*

For the love of all things wil
For the heart of the unbo
Give us all the will to nurtu
Give them all a certain fut

$\mathscr{A}$LL THINGS WILD

This special child's sampler is dedicated to my children, James and Louise. This delightful sampler depicting children's favourite wild animals would make a lovely gift to a new son, daughter or even grandchild!

SKILL LEVEL 3
STITCH COUNT: 285 × 157
DESIGN SIZE: 20¼ × 11¼ in (51.5 × 28.5 cm)

~

MATERIALS
25½ × 16¼ in (65 × 41 cm) Jobelan fabric
(Article 449, shade 16), 28 threads to 1 in (2.5 cm)
Stranded cottons (floss) as listed on the chart
Tapestry needle size 26
A purchased frame

1. Fold the fabric in four, press lightly and mark the folds with a line of tacking (basting) stitches, beginning at the left of a vertical thread (see Where and How to Start, page 12).

2. Follow the chart on pages 38–39 and stitch the design using two strands of stranded cotton (floss) for the cross stitch and one strand for the backstitch outline.

3. When complete, check for missed stitches, and press lightly on the wrong side. Stretch and frame as preferred (see page 126).

~

Children love animals and here twelve creatures of the wild surround a poem dedicated to them. This special children's sampler would make a lovely gift, to be treasured for years to come.

CHILDHOOD TREASURES

*Here are two delightful projects to welcome your
child. The Christening Sampler will be treasured long after the event
and will act as a reminder of a happy day, shared by friends and family.
This small, intricate, mini-band sampler commemorates the location of your child's
christening or alternatively you could substitute the date of the occasion. It will give you the
chance to try some new counted stitches as well as a delicate panel of cutwork. The
cutwork section (photographed in detail below) is not difficult, but could
be omitted if preferred! For the second project, work only the cross
to produce an attractive card for a child's confirmation.*

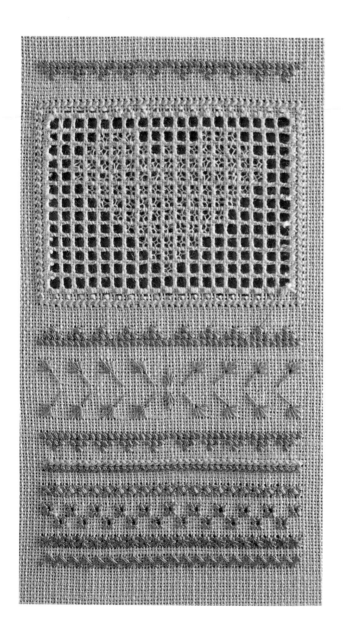

CHRISTENING SAMPLER

All the new stitches included in this sampler are
illustrated in Additional Stitches, page 14,
although I have included the cutwork diagrams
here. Looking at the charts on pages 44 and 45,
you will see that each band is numbered (1 to 15)
with a list of techniques used listed below.

SKILL LEVEL 5
STITCH COUNT: 43 × 169
DESIGN SIZE: 3 × 12 in (7.5 × 30 cm)

~

MATERIALS
6 × 16 in (15 × 40.5 cm) Jobelan fabric
(Article 449, shade 26), 28 threads to 1 in (2.5 cm)
Stranded cottons (floss) as listed on the chart
Madeira metallic thread, gold 22
Tapestry needle size 26

1. Fold the fabric in four, press lightly and mark
the folds with a line of tacking (basting) stitches,
beginning to the left of a vertical thread (see Where
and How to Start, page 12).

~

Left: *Detail of the cutwork panel.*
Opposite: *The Christening Sampler.*

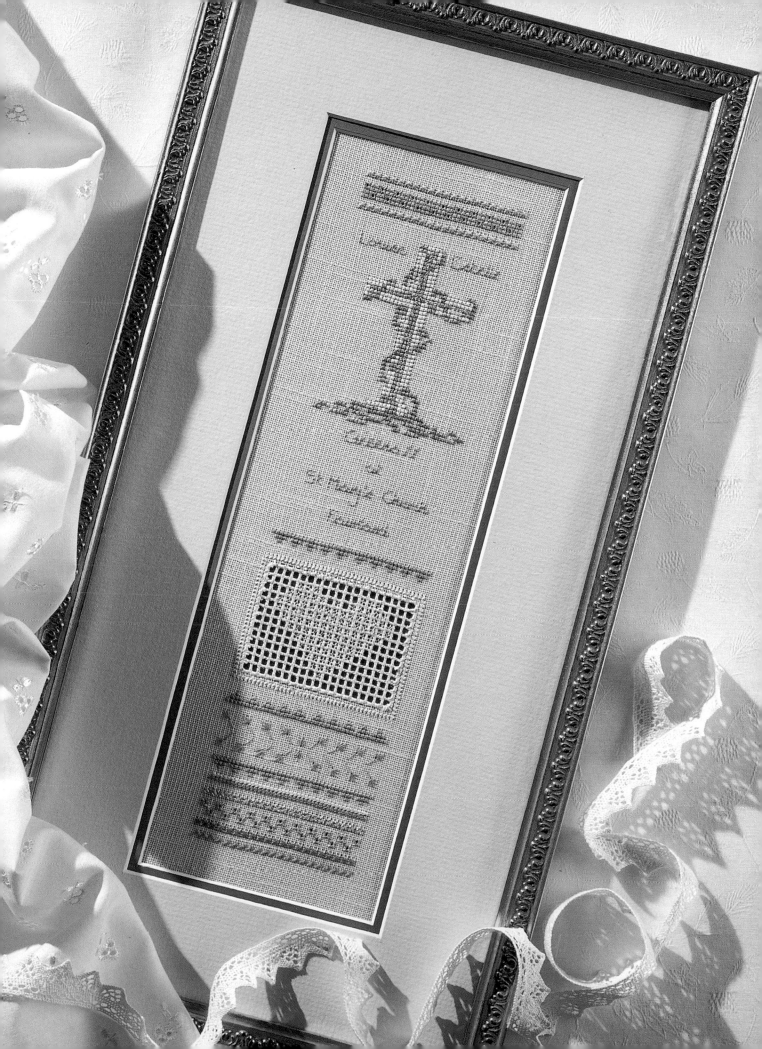

2. Following the charts on pages 44 and 45, and referring to the list of techniques, count to the dove's eye cutwork heart first. Using two strands of stranded cotton (floss), work the hemstitch around the cutwork area. Take care to count this section carefully, referring to the chart if you are not sure.

3. The next step is to cut the threads. Count to the centre of the hemmed area and carefully snip alternate sets of two threads across and down (see fig 26) using very sharp pointed scissors. This will leave the open section to be decorated looking something like fig 26.

Fig 26 Snip alternate sets of two threads across and down, and tack out of the way

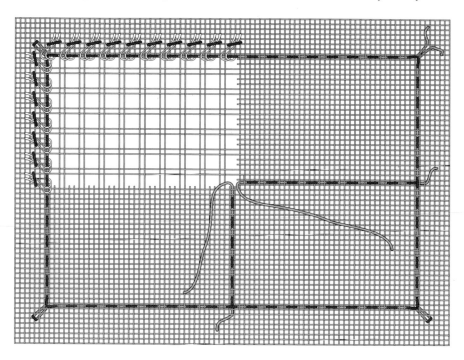

Fig 27 Chart showing the pairs of threads which are cut and which are left in position

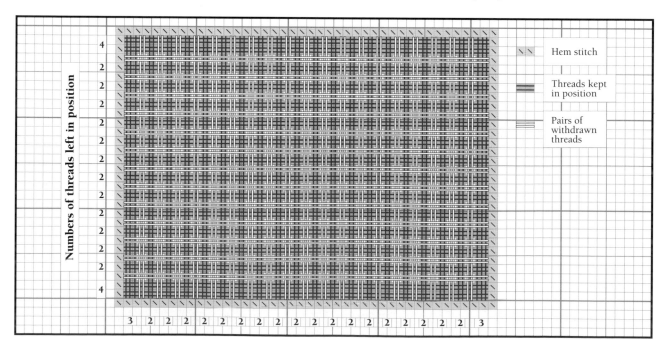

4. Carefully unravel the cut threads from the middle to the hemstitched edge, leaving a two-thread border at the sides and three threads at the top and bottom (see fig 27). On the back of the work, loosely tack (baste) these threads out of the way. They will be dealt with later (see fig 26).

5. Working on the horizontal bars first, stitching from left to right and using one strand of stranded cotton (floss), wrap each bar twice (see fig 28), turning the work at the end of each section. *Stitching Tip:* Start and finish at the end of each section. Do not begin a new thread in the middle of a row.

6. Work the vertical bars next, adding dove's eye stitches in the marked squares (see chart).

7. Continue until the heart motif is complete. Now, using two strands of stranded cotton (floss), work satin stitch around the edge, between the cutwork and the hemstitched border. Take a pair of sharp, pointed scissors and carefully cut away the loose threads.

8. To stitch the remaining bands, use two strands of stranded cotton (floss) for the cross stitch and one strand for the backstitch, following the chart and referring to the chart key. *Stitching Tip:* When using metallic threads, use short lengths to help prevent the tangles and twists that can occur.

9. Finish loose ends and stretch and frame as preferred (see page 126).

Fig 28 Wrapping the bars. Add dove's eye stitches in the marked squares as the vertical bars are worked.

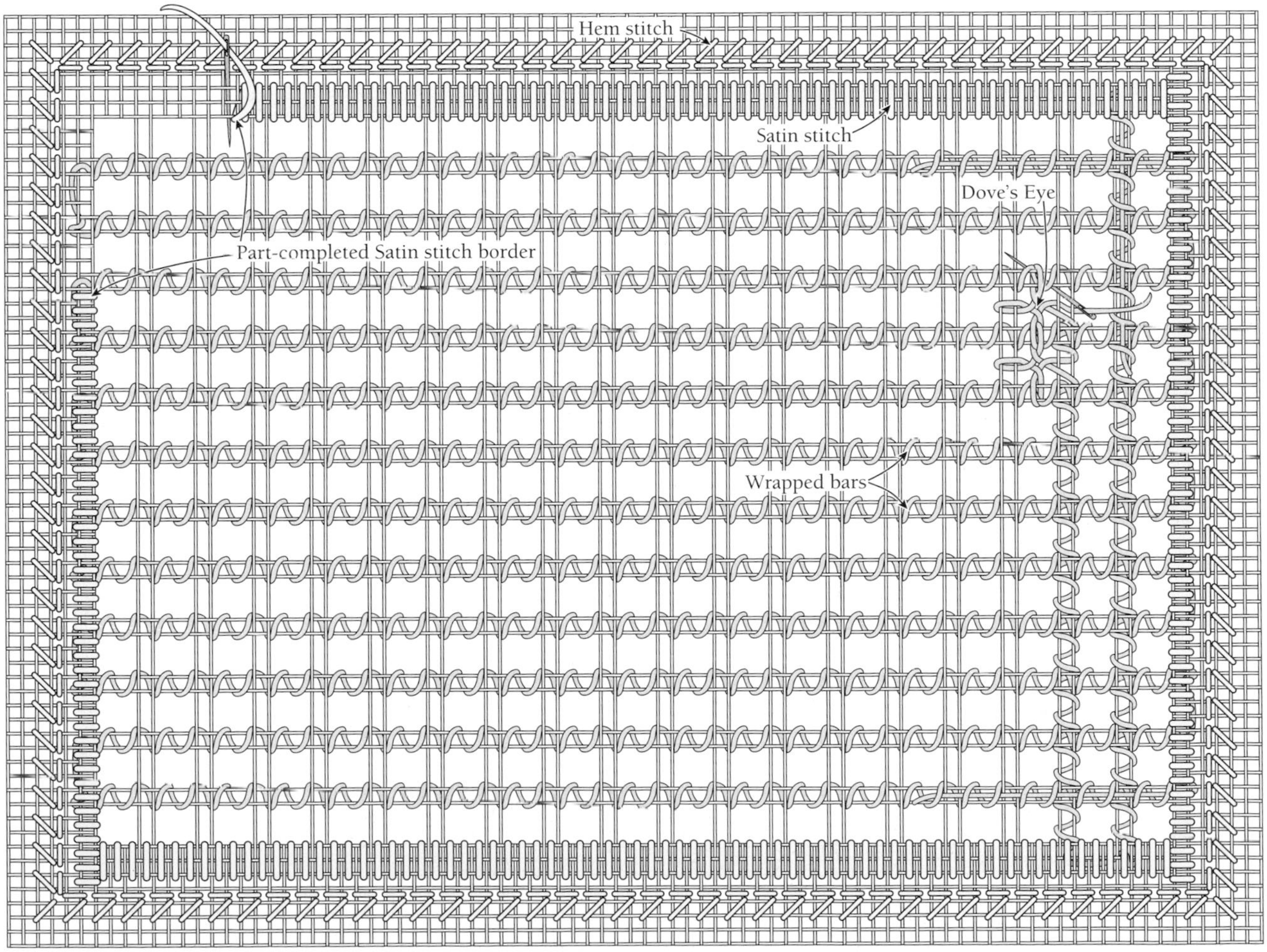

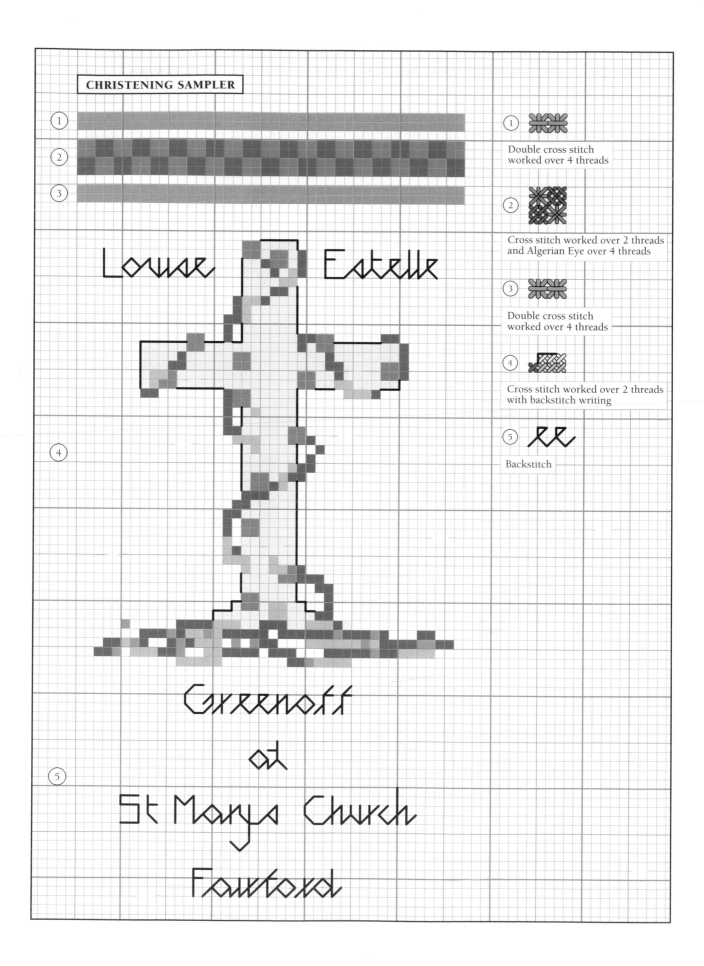

CHRISTENING SAMPLER

① Double cross stitch worked over 4 threads

② Cross stitch worked over 2 threads and Algerian Eye over 4 threads

③ Double cross stitch worked over 4 threads

④ Cross stitch worked over 2 threads with backstitch writing

⑤ Backstitch

Louise   Estelle

Greenoff

at

St Marys Church

Fairford

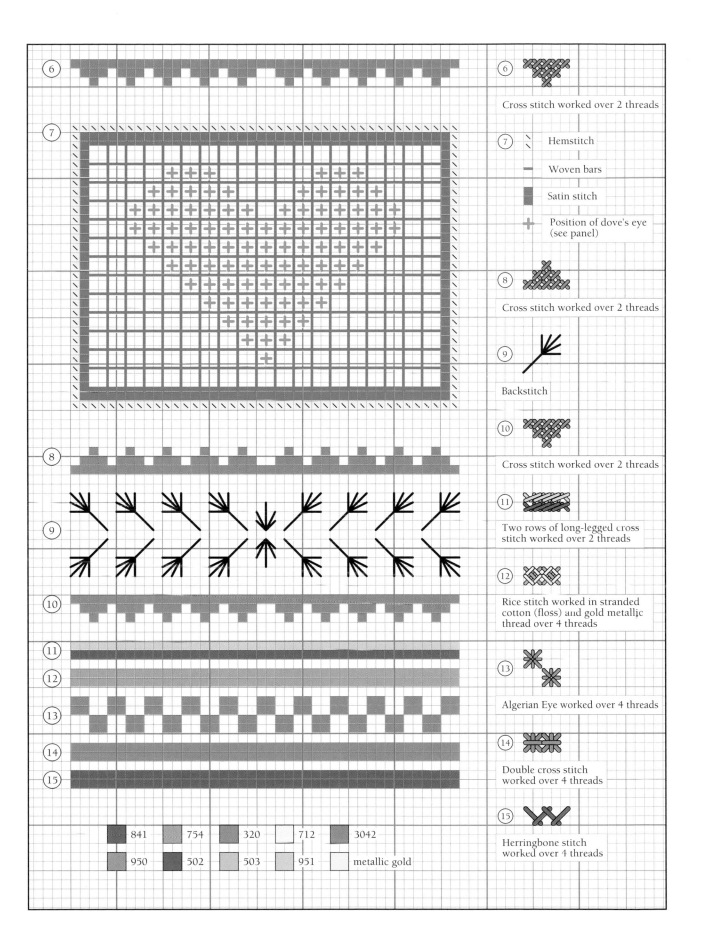

(6) Cross stitch worked over 2 threads

(7)
⟍ Hemstitch
— Woven bars
▬ Satin stitch
✛ Position of dove's eye (see panel)

(8) Cross stitch worked over 2 threads

(9) Backstitch

(10) Cross stitch worked over 2 threads

(11) Two rows of long-legged cross stitch worked over 2 threads

(12) Rice stitch worked in stranded cotton (floss) and gold metallic thread over 4 threads

(13) Algerian Eye worked over 4 threads

(14) Double cross stitch worked over 4 threads

(15) Herringbone stitch worked over 4 threads

	841		754		320		712		3042
	950		502		503		951		metallic gold

CONFIRMATION CARD

This simple design, taken from the Christening Sampler, is stitched on Aida fabric and added to a three-fold card (see Suppliers, page 133).

This simple design of a cross interwoven with leaves makes an attractive Confirmation Card. The design has been taken from the Christening Sampler shown on page 41.

SKILL LEVEL 1
STITCH COUNT: 39 × 46
DESIGN SIZE: 3 × 3½ in (7.5 × 9 cm)

MATERIALS
5 × 6 in (12.5 × 15 cm) Zweigart Aida, shade 323, 14 blocks to 1 in (2.5 cm)

Stranded cottons (floss) as listed on the chart

Tapestry needle size 24

One arched three-fold card

¾ yd (75 cm) cream satin ribbon to trim

Double-sided adhesive tape

1. Fold the fabric in four, press lightly and mark the folds with a line of tacking (basting) stitches.

2. Following the chart on page 44, stitch the design using two strands of stranded cotton (floss) for the cross stitch and one strand for the backstitch outline.

3. When the project is complete, check for missed stitches, press lightly on the wrong side and make up as described on page 127.

$\mathcal{B}$ALLOON CELEBRATION

This fun section of the book allows you to design and adapt the charts to suit your chosen celebration. It features balloon projects which can be used for almost any event! I have used the balloon charts on pages 50 and 51 to produce a Happy Birthday Sampler (page 49), a Congratulations Banner and a 'Well Done' Message Board (pictured below).

HAPPY BIRTHDAY SAMPLER

This project is intended as a family birthday card and would look good hung in a position of honour with streamers and balloons attached. Relevant photographs and special cards may be attached to the bottom as shown in the photograph. My example includes a border of long-legged and double cross stitch and heart-shaped Hardanger balloons. If you intend to copy the version illustrated, you will need to use evenweave fabric and not Aida (see page 9). If preferred, these heart-shaped balloons may be stitched in cross stitch on Aida.

SKILL LEVEL 5
STITCH COUNT: 102 × 130
DESIGN SIZE: 7¼ × 9¼ in (18.5 × 23 cm)
~
MATERIALS
12½ × 13½ in (32 × 34 cm) Jobelan fabric
(Article 429, shade 24), 28 threads to 1 in (2.5 cm)

Stranded cottons (floss) as listed on the chart

DMC Perlé 8 in cream

DMC Perlé 12 in cream

Tapestry needle size 26 and 22

12½ × 13½ in (32 × 34 cm) blue fabric for the background

A purchased frame

Four small brass cup hooks

Four 8 in (20 cm) lengths of blue ribbon to attach cards

1. Fold the fabric in four, press lightly and mark the folds with a line of tacking (basting) stitches, beginning at the left of a vertical thread (see Where and How to Start, page 12).

2. Starting at the left of a vertical thread, work the cross stitch from the chart on pages 50 and 51, using two strands of stranded cotton (floss) for the cross stitch and one strand for the backstitch balloon strings.

3. In the example illustrated on page 49, I have worked the three heart-shaped balloons using

~

Above: *Detail of the heart-shaped balloon from the Happy Birthday Sampler which is pictured on the opposite page.*

Hardanger technique. See pages 13 and 14 for instructions on kloster blocks and dove's eye stitch before starting to stitch. Work the kloster blocks for the three balloons first, cut the threads and then needleweave the loose bars, adding the dove's eye stitches as illustrated on page 14.

4. When the balloon design is complete, work the long-legged and double cross stitch border as follows. Following the chart, work the long-legged cross stitch using two strands of stranded cotton (floss) over two threads of fabric. Add the double cross stitch using two strands of stranded cotton (floss) over four threads (see Additional Stitches, page 14).

5. When the design is complete, check for missed stitches and press on the wrong side. To complete the project, line the stitching with the blue backing fabric and frame as illustrated. Then add four small brass cup hooks to the bottom of the frame so that you can hang photographs or cards on the lengths of ribbon.

BALLOON CELEBRATION

3750	791	3746	3350	931	3687	3341	LL Long-legged cross stitch
3820	3803	340	3823	793	3705	3747	

For You

Celebration

Hurrah!

A Boy! A Girl!

Well Done!

Congratulations

Let's Celebrate

How Lovely!

Kloster Blocks

Kloster Blocks

Kloster Blocks

Happy Birthday!

Double cross stitch over 4 threads

LL

LL

LL

LL

CONGRATULATIONS BANNER

Whatever the occasion, from a special birthday to the passing of a driving test, from the birth of a baby, to the engagement of a happy couple, this picture (on page 47) will help you to get across your message of congratulations in a unique and novel way. This design uses the balloons and text from the charts on pages 50 and 51, but with one balloon stitched on silver Stitching Paper and appliquéd using backstitch.

SKILL LEVEL 3
STITCH COUNT: 113 × 56
DESIGN SIZE: 8 × 4 in (20 × 10 cm)

~

MATERIALS
8 × 10½ in (20 × 26.5 cm) Jobelan fabric
(Article 429, shade 41), 28 threads to 1 in (2.5 cm)
Stranded cottons (floss) as listed on the chart
2½ in (6.25 cm) square silver Stitching Paper
Tapestry needle size 26
Graph paper and pencil
A purchased frame

1. Fold the fabric in four, press lightly and mark the folds with a line of tacking (basting) stitches, beginning at the left of a vertical thread (see Where and How to Start, page 12).

2. Using the graph paper and pencil, copy the outline of the text you have selected from the chart on page 50, and add a selection of balloons as shown in the illustration on page 49 (see Planning Layout Charts, page 8). Leave a space for the Stitching Paper balloon which can be added at the end.

3. Starting at the left of a vertical thread, work the cross stitch from the charts on pages 50 and 51, using two strands of stranded cotton (floss) for the cross stitch and one strand for the backstitch balloon strings. When complete, press lightly on the wrong side and set aside.

4. Work the heart-shaped balloon on a piece of Stitching Paper, using three strands of stranded cotton (floss) for the cross stitch (see page 10).

5. Using a small pair of pointed scissors, carefully cut out the balloon, leaving a narrow margin. Position the balloon on the stitching and attach, using two strands of stranded cotton (floss), then backstitch around the edge. When complete, stretch and finish as preferred.

'WELL DONE' MESSAGE BOARD

This easy-to-complete project is ideal for a child's room, although the fabric requirements will need to be adapted if you do not use the same novelty blackboard frame shown here.

SKILL LEVEL 1
STITCH COUNT: 53 × 84
DESIGN SIZE: 4 × 6¼ in (10 × 16 cm)

~

MATERIALS
8 × 12 in (20.5 × 30.5 cm) Zweigart Aida, shade 713,
14 blocks to 1 in (2.5 cm)
Stranded cottons (floss) as listed on the chart
Tapestry needle size 24
Purchased message board (see Suppliers, page 133)

1. Fold the fabric in four, press lightly and mark folds with a line of tacking (basting) stitches.

2. Plan the layout as for the Congratulations Banner (see step 2).

3. Starting in the middle, work the cross stitch following the charts on pages 50 and 51, using two strands of stranded cotton (floss) for the cross stitch and one strand for the backstitch balloon strings.

4. When the design is complete, stretch and make up following the manufacturer's instructions.

BIRTHDAY GREETINGS

This selection of birthday greetings cards will give you lots of ways to wish family and friends many happy returns of the day. The Decorative Number cards use three very different styles of charted numerals to suit a wide range of tastes and ages, while the two cards charted for It Was a Very Good Year celebrate the year of birth and provide a choice of two floral borders.

DECORATIVE NUMBER CARDS

The number charts on pages 54 and 55 are ideal to adapt for a particularly special birthday or even anniversary. You can combine the numbers to form cards as illustrated below or mix and match to make dates.

I have not included specific instructions for stitching these cards as they will all vary depending on the celebration you require them for.

However, you might like to know that the examples in the colour photograph were stitched on the following fabrics:
'90' on Yorkshire Aida, 14 blocks to 1 in (2.5 cm)
'?!39' on Zweigart Aida (shade 264), 16 blocks to 1 in (2.5 cm)
'40' on Zweigart Aida 14 (shade 309), 14 blocks to 1 in (2.5 cm)

Once your stitching is complete, press lightly and make up into three fold cards (see page 127).

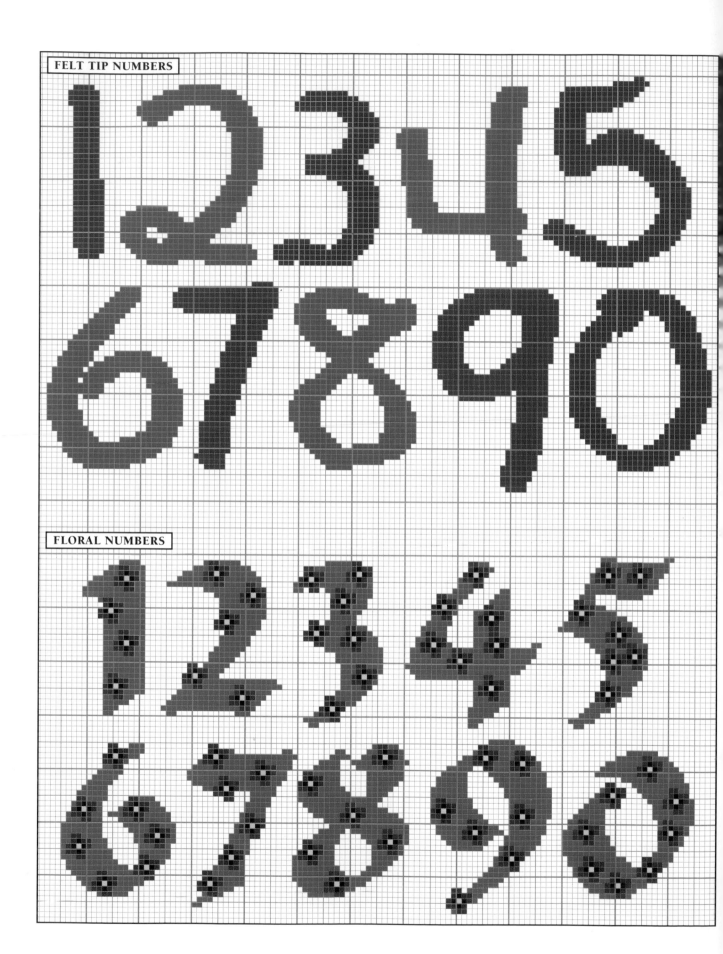

FELT TIP NUMBERS

FLORAL NUMBERS

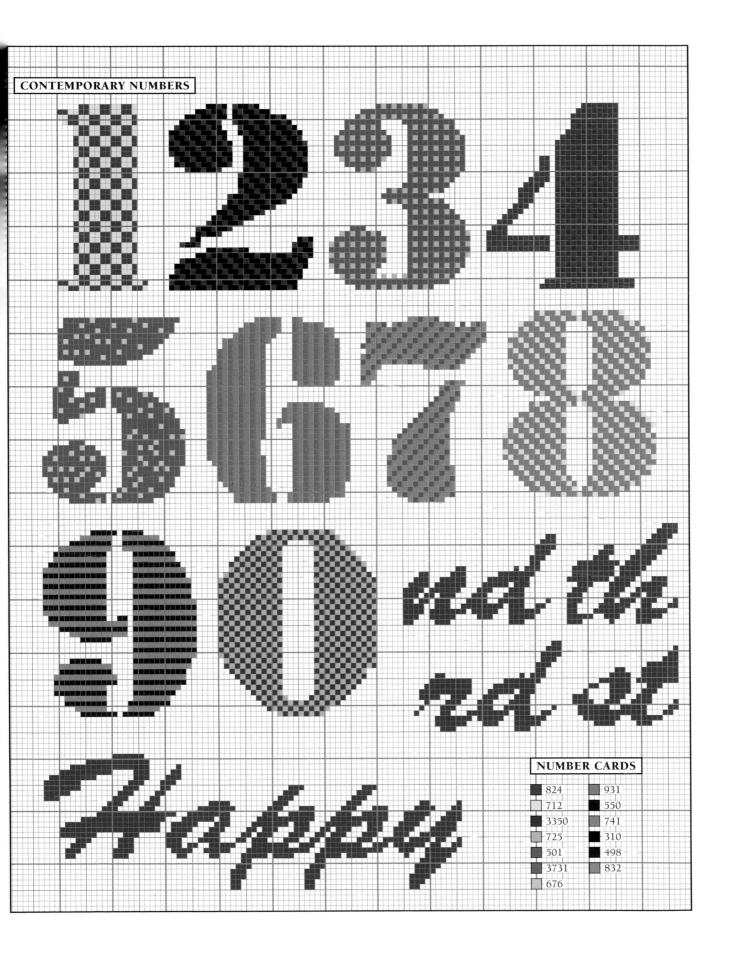

NUMBER CARDS

■	824		931
	712	■	550
■	3350		741
	725	■	310
	501	■	498
	3731		832
	676		

IT WAS A VERY GOOD YEAR!

For these two unusual birthday cards I treated the fabric and one of the cards with spray paint before the projects were stitched. The paint used was a non-metallic car paint bought from a car accessory shop. One of the purchased three-fold cards was lightly sprayed with green paint and glitter spray paint before making up.

As both designs are constructed in the same way, I have given the instructions for one only.

SKILL LEVEL 1
STITCH COUNT: Tulip 123 × 65; Poppy 138 × 83
DESIGN SIZE: Tulip 7¾ × 4 in (20 × 10 cm);
Poppy 8¾ × 5¾ in (22 × 13.5 cm)

~

MATERIALS
8 × 10 in (20 × 25 cm) Zweigart Aida, shade 264,
16 blocks to 1 in (2.5 cm)
Stranded cottons (floss) as listed on the chart
Tapestry needle size 26
One can of spray paint (Ford Laurel Green) for the fabric
One can of spray paint (Vauxhall Jade) for one card
One can of Do It Glitter spray (gold shade 584)
Graph paper and pencil
A purchased three-fold card
Two 8 in (20.5 cm) lengths of silk ribbon

1. Before beginning to stitch the design, the fabric is sprayed with paint and left to dry overnight. To do this, first iron the Aida fabric firmly to ensure that all folds and creases are removed. Cover a flat surface with paper because the spray paint goes everywhere! Place the fabric in the middle of the protective paper and shake the paint can for about three minutes. Practise with the spray on paper first because it is important to use a light spray without drips or blotches. Once sprayed, leave the fabric on a flat surface to dry before treating in the normal way.

2. Before starting the card, select the border you prefer from the charts on pages 58 and 59, and draw a simple outline on the graph paper (see Planning Layout Charts, page 8). Choose the numbers you require and add them to the chart. Centre the chart and check your stitch count. Adapt your fabric requirements if your stitch count varies from mine.

3. Fold the fabric in four, press lightly and mark the folds with a line of tacking (basting) stitches. Starting in the middle, work the cross stitch by following the charts on pages 58 or 59 and your layout chart. Use two strands of stranded cotton (floss) for the cross stitch and one strand for the backstitch outline.

4. When complete, press lightly on the wrong side and make up as described on page 128.

~

Below: *Detail from the poppy design.*
Right: *Celebrate someone special's birthday with these unusual cards.*

BEADED LILY WEDDING SAMPLER

The addition of small glass beads to the tips of the lily stamens makes this exquisite wedding sampler extra special.

SKILL LEVEL 3
STITCH COUNT: 210 × 148
DESIGN SIZE: 15 × 10½ in (38 × 26.5 cm)
~
MATERIALS
20 × 15¼ in (51 × 39 cm) Jobelan fabric
(Article 429, shade 131), 28 threads to 1 in (2.5 cm)
Stranded cottons (floss) as listed on the chart
Tapestry needle size 26
One pack Mill Hill Glass Seed Beads, shade 00275
Sharp or beading needle size 12
A purchased frame

1. Fold the fabric in four, press lightly and mark the folds with tacking (basting) stitches. If working on an evenweave fabric, remember to begin tacking to the left of a vertical thread.

2. Following the charts on pages 62 and 63, start in the centre and work the design using two strands of stranded cotton (floss) for the cross stitch. The roof of the church is tweeded with two shades of grey in the needle (see Tweeding, page 13). Add the backstitch to the church and lily border using one strand of stranded cotton (floss).

3. Add the stamens on each lily using a single long stitch and one strand of stranded cotton (floss). Add a bead to each stamen using a sharp needle, a half cross stitch and matching thread.

4. When complete, check for missed stitches and stretch and frame as desired (see page 126).

MAGNOLIA WEDDING

These two pretty cross stitch wedding designs include some simple Hardanger embroidery stitches and techniques. Before beginning either project, read the Hardanger instructions on page 13; and if this is your first attempt at Hardanger you might find it easier to make the Bride's Garter Pocket project first (see page 66).

RING PILLOW

This gorgeous ring pillow would make a delightful gift for any couple starting out in life together. It is piped and finished in silk dupion, and the wedding rings are attached by matching ribbon bows, and provides a lasting momento of a special day.
Note: The stitch count below refers to the number of blocks occupied by the straight stitches forming the kloster blocks. The example illustrated is stitched on an evenweave fabric but Hardanger could be substituted.

SKILL LEVEL 5
STITCH COUNT: 85 × 90
DESIGN SIZE: 5¼ × 5½ in (13.5 × 14 cm)

MATERIALS
10 in (25.5 cm) square Jobelan fabric
(Article 429, shade 120), 28 threads to 1 in (2.5 cm)
Stranded cottons (floss) as listed on the chart
DMC Perlé 8 in Ecru
DMC Perlé 12 in Ecru
Tapestry needle size 26 and 22
8 in (20.5 cm) square silk dupion for the backing
(colour of your choosing)
20 in (50 cm) length piping cord
10 in (25.5 cm) pale peach silk dupion for contrast piping

1. Fold the fabric in four, press lightly and mark the folds with tacking (basting) stitches, beginning to the left of a vertical thread (see Where and How to Start, page 12).

2. Starting to the left of a vertical thread work the cross stitch from the chart on page 67, using two strands of stranded cotton (floss) for the cross stitch and one strand for the backstitch outline.

3. When the magnolia motif is complete, work the kloster blocks as shown on the chart, using one strand of Perlé 8. Remember each block is made up of *five* straight stitches, all of which are worked over four threads. As you stitch, keep checking that every kloster block has a similar block directly opposite. When all the blocks are complete, check for any loose ends and any miscounts.

4. Work the eyelet stitches in two strands of stranded cotton (floss) in the colour indicated on the chart, adding any initials or dates as desired (see the charts on pages 124 and 125 for more alphabets and numbers).

5. When all the cross stitch, kloster blocks and eyelet stitches are completed, cut the threads at the end of the kloster blocks as shown on the chart. Use a small pair of sharp, pointed scissors and cut one section at a time, withdraw the cut threads and then, following the chart, needleweave the bars as illustrated, adding dove's eye stitches as you complete each section.

Opposite: The romantic lacy designs of the Bride's Garter Pocket and the Wedding Ring Pillow.

A NEW BEGINNING

This distinctive rose design is illustrated in two colourways as can be seen opposite and is simple to adapt to suit an engagement, wedding or anniversary.

RED ROSE PICTURE

This striking design would be particularly suitable for a ruby wedding anniversary gift, or as a wedding present for a couple who have found happiness the second time around.

SKILL LEVEL: 1
STITCH COUNT: 99 × 121
DESIGN SIZE: 8 × 9½ in (20 × 24 cm)

~

MATERIALS
12½ × 14½ in (32 × 37 cm) mint-green linen,
25 threads to 1 in (2.5 cm)
Stranded cottons (floss) as listed on the chart
Tapestry needle size 24
A purchased frame

1. Fold the fabric in four, press lightly and mark the folds with tacking (basting) stitches. If working on an evenweave fabric, remember to begin tacking to the left of a vertical thread (see Where and How to Start, page 12).

2. Following the chart on pages 70 and 71 and starting in the centre, work the cross stitch using two strands of stranded cotton (floss), remembering to keep the top stitches facing in the same direction. Add any optional outline in backstitch, using one strand of the colour indicated on the chart.

3. When complete, check for missed stitches and press lightly on the wrong side. Stretch and frame as preferred (see page 126).

IVORY ROSE OVAL

This attractive rose picture has been stitched from the charts on pages 70 and 71 and a small heart charm has been attached with ivory silk ribbon.

SKILL LEVEL 3
STITCH COUNT: 97 × 122
DESIGN SIZE: 7½ × 9½ in (19 × 24 cm)

~

MATERIALS
12 × 14 in (30.5 × 35.5 cm) unbleached linen,
26 threads to 1 in (2.5 cm)
Stranded cottons (floss) as listed in brackets on the chart
Tapestry needle size 26
A purchased gold coloured oval frame
Gold coloured heart-shaped charm (optional)
10 in (25 cm) cream satin ribbon (optional)

1. Fold the fabric in four, press lightly and mark the folds with tacking (basting) stitches. If working on an evenweave fabric, remember to begin tacking to the left of a vertical thread (see Where and How to Start, page 12).

2. Following the chart on page 71 and starting in the centre, work the cross stitch using two strands of stranded cotton (floss). Add any optional outline in backstitch using one strand of the colour indicated on the chart.

3. Check for missed stitches, press lightly on the wrong side and attach the optional charm using matching thread and the satin ribbon. Stretch and frame (see page 126).

With
Love
on our
Anniversa

A New
Begin

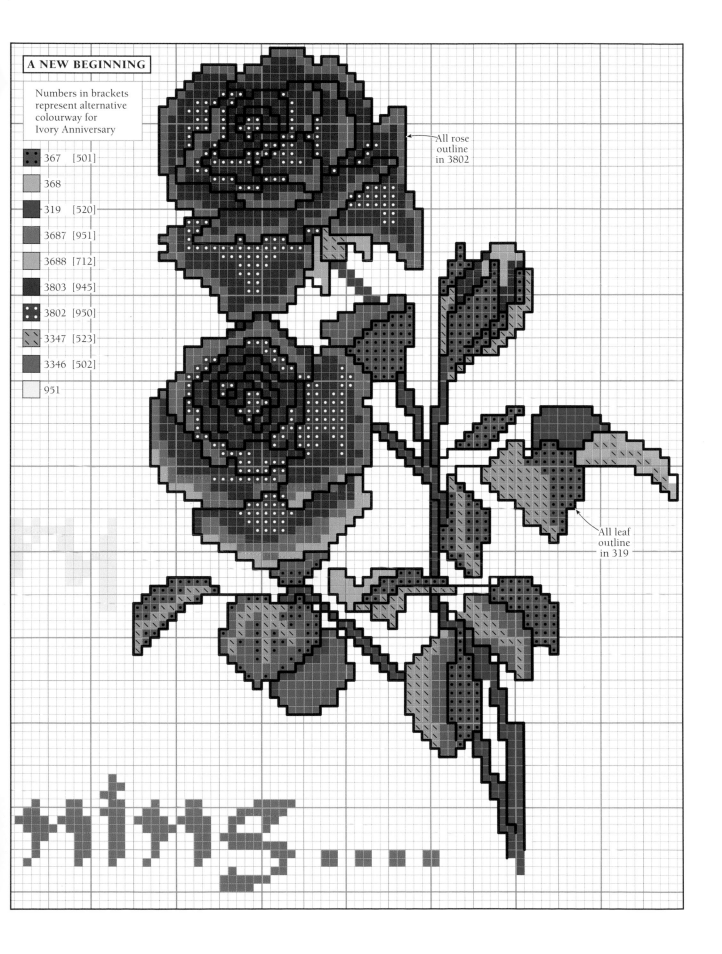

A NEW BEGINNING

Numbers in brackets represent alternative colourway for Ivory Anniversary

- 367 [501]
- 368
- 319 [520]
- 3687 [951]
- 3688 [712]
- 3803 [945]
- 3802 [950]
- 3347 [523]
- 3346 [502]
- 951

All rose outline in 3802

All leaf outline in 319

 SPECIAL DAY

*This lovely sampler design with its exquisite floral
border would be perfect for a number of special days,
including an engagement or a wedding. I have lifted the
rose motif from the sampler chart to produce two
special gifts – a card and a trinket box lid.*

THE SAMPLER

The project was stitched on pure linen but would
also suit Aida if preferred.

SKILL LEVEL 4
STITCH COUNT: 203 × 257
DESIGN SIZE: 14½ × 18½ in (37 × 47 cm)
~
MATERIALS
19½ × 23½ in (49.5 × 60 cm) violet linen,
28 threads to 1 in (2.5 cm)
Stranded cottons (floss) as listed on the chart
Tapestry needle size 26
A purchased frame

1. Fold the fabric in four, press lightly and mark
the folds with a line of tacking (basting) stitches,
beginning at the left of a vertical thread (see Where
and How to Start, page 12).

2. Starting at the left of a vertical thread, work the
cross stitch from the charts on pages 74–77,
using two strands of stranded cotton (floss) for the
cross stitch and one strand for the backstitch
outline. Add the stamens to the passion flower
using one strand of stranded cotton (floss) and
long stitches.

3. When the design is complete, check for missed
stitches and press lightly on the wrong side.
Stretch and frame as desired (see page 126).

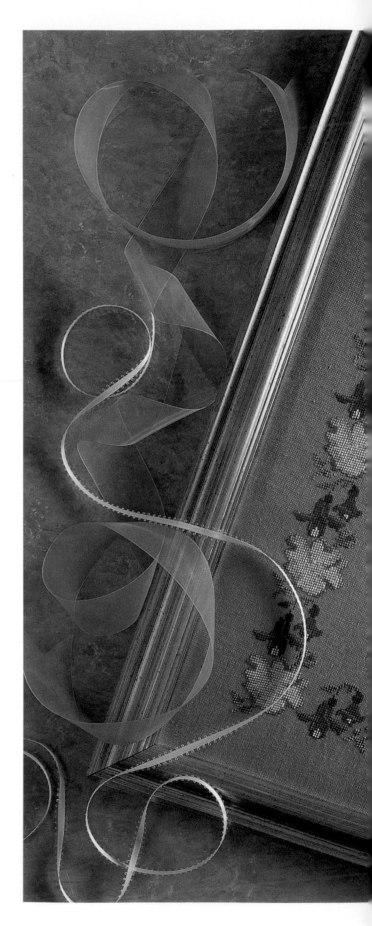

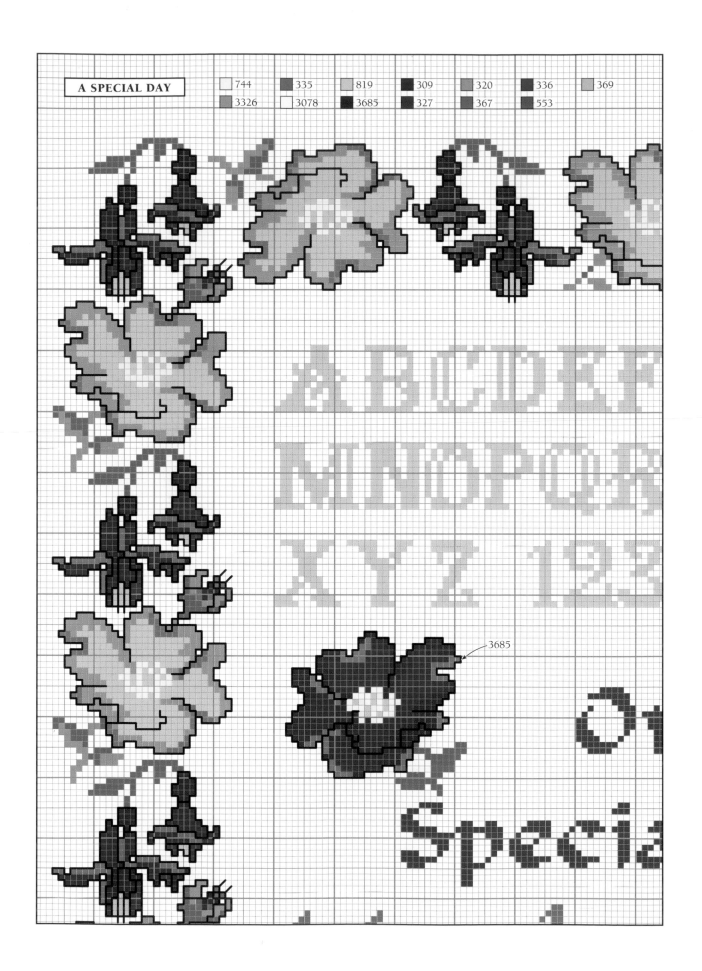

A SPECIAL DAY

| 744 | 335 | 819 | 309 | 320 | 336 | 369 |
| 3326 | 3078 | 3685 | 327 | 367 | 553 | |

3685

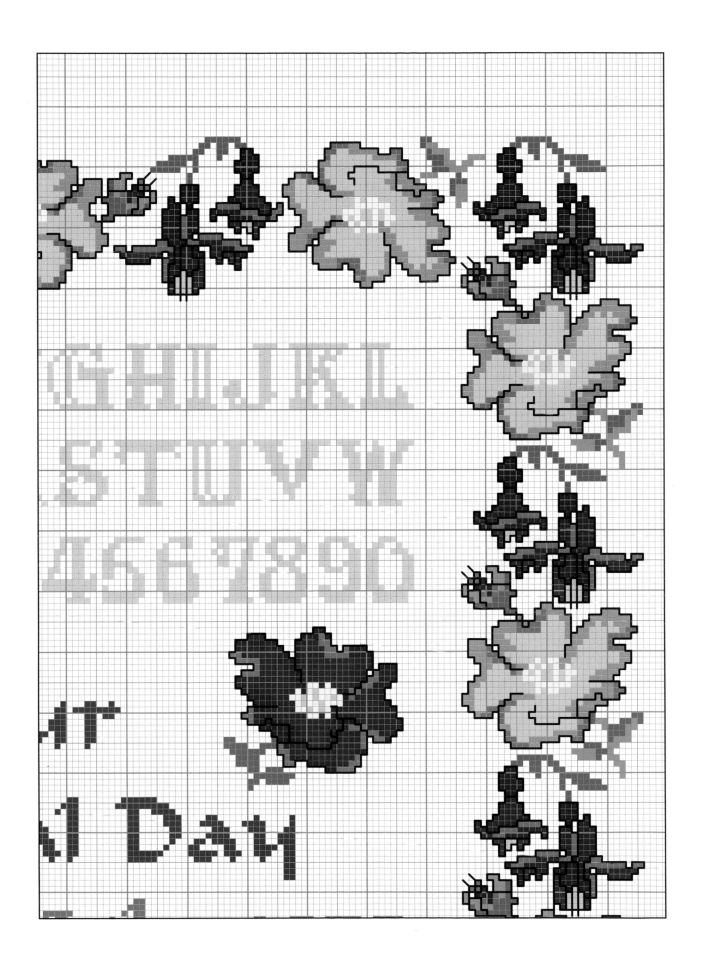

367

A SPECIAL DAY (continued)		744		335		819		309		320		336		369
		3326		3078		3685		327		367		553		

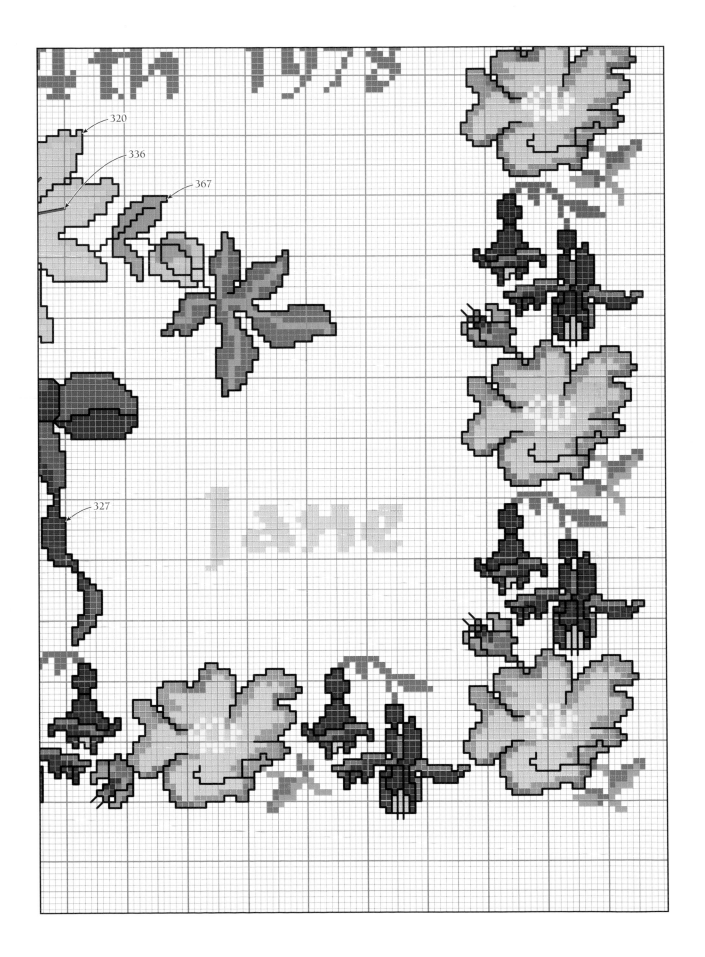

WILD ROSE TRINKET POT

A single wild rose worked on linen and added to a round trinket box makes a perfect gift. Work this motif (taken from the Special Day chart) on Aida for a Skill Level 1 project.

SKILL LEVEL 3
STITCH COUNT: 27 × 29
DESIGN SIZE: 2¼ in (5.5 cm) diameter (approx)

~

MATERIALS
5 in (12.5 cm) mint-green linen,
25 threads to 1 in (2.5 cm)
Stranded cottons (floss) as listed on the chart
Tapestry needle size 24
A round Framecraft trinket pot, 3 in (7.5 cm)
diameter (see Suppliers, page 133)

1. Fold the fabric in four, press lightly and mark the folds with a line of tacking (basting) stitches,

~

*The single wild rose motif can
be taken from the Special Day chart and worked
to produce smaller items.*

beginning at the left of a vertical thread (see Where and How to Start, page 12).

2. Following the chart on pages 74–75, using two strands of stranded cotton (floss) for the cross stitch and one strand for the backstitch outline, work the rose motif.

3. When the cross stitch is complete, press lightly and make up as instructed by the manufacturers.

WILD ROSE CARD

I have used the same rose motif as for the Wild Rose Trinket Pot but this time working it on gold Stitching Paper set within a three-fold card.

SKILL LEVEL 1
STITCH COUNT: 29 × 27
DESIGN SIZE: 2 × 2 in (5 × 5 cm)

~

MATERIALS
4 × 5 in (10 × 12.5 cm) gold Stitching Paper
Stranded cottons (floss) as listed on the chart
Tapestry needle size 24
One heart-shaped three-fold card (see Suppliers, page 133)
Double-sided adhesive tape
20 in (50 cm) lengths each pale pink and
cerise satin ribbon

Before starting to stitch on Stitching Paper, refer to page 10 for basic techniques.

1. Following the chart on pages 74–75 and working from the centre of the rose motif, stitch the cross stitch using three strands of stranded cotton (floss) for the cross stitch and two strands for the backstitch outline.

2. When the design is complete, check for missed stitches and make up as described on page 128. Add the ribbon trim as desired.

PASSION FLOWER HORSESHOE

This exquisite gift for a special bride was the brainchild of a friend, who designed a lily horseshoe
for her daughter. The completed project is padded and decorated with small seed pearls.

SKILL LEVEL 4
STITCH COUNT: 144 × 125
DESIGN SIZE: 8 × 7 in (20 × 18 cm)

~

MATERIALS

12 in (30.5 cm) square cream linen,
36 threads to 1 in (2.5 cm)

Stranded cottons (floss) as listed on the chart

Tapestry needle size 26

11 in (28 cm) square piece of foam core

12 in (30.5 cm) square cream silk dupion fabric

Polyester wadding (batting)

Double-sided adhesive tape

Approximately 100 seed pearls

Sharp or beading needle

Two small silk roses (optional)

39½ in (1 m) cream satin ribbon (optional)

1. Fold the fabric in four, press lightly and mark the folds with a line of tacking (basting) stitches, beginning at the left of a vertical thread (see Where and How to Start, page 12).

~

A detail from the bride's horseshoe showing a single passion flower which has been worked on cream linen in delicate colours.

2. Starting at the left of a vertical thread, work the cross stitch from the chart opposite, using two strands of stranded cotton (floss) for the cross stitch and one strand for the backstitch. Add the flower stamens with one long stitch in a single strand. When complete, press on the wrong side and set aside.

3. Using the template provided on page 131, cut a tracing paper pattern for the horseshoe. Then, using a sharp craft knife, cut out a horseshoe shape for the foam core.

4. Placing the paper pattern on top of your stitching, carefully cut out the horseshoe shape, checking that the stitching is in the right position and adding at least 1½ in (4 cm) for turnings. Then, using your stitching as a pattern, cut a second horseshoe shape from the silk dupion fabric for the backing.

5. Using a little double-sided adhesive tape, cover the foam core with one layer of polyester wadding (batting) and trim the wadding to shape. Then, position the stitching on top of the covered foam core and using glass-headed pins, pin the stitching around the edge, gently smoothing out any wrinkles and gathers as you go (see Stretching and Framing, page 126). When you are satisfied with the appearance, apply strips of double-sided adhesive tape to the back of the foam core and fold under the excess fabric, sticking in place.

6. Remove all the pins and lay the stitching face down on a clean, flat surface. Folding under the raw edges as you go, pin the silk dupion fabric to the back and slip stitch together invisibly.

7. Using a sharp or beading needle, matching thread and a half cross stitch, add the seed pearls at regular intervals around the edge.

8. Trim with silk roses and ribbons as desired. Add a ribbon hanger.

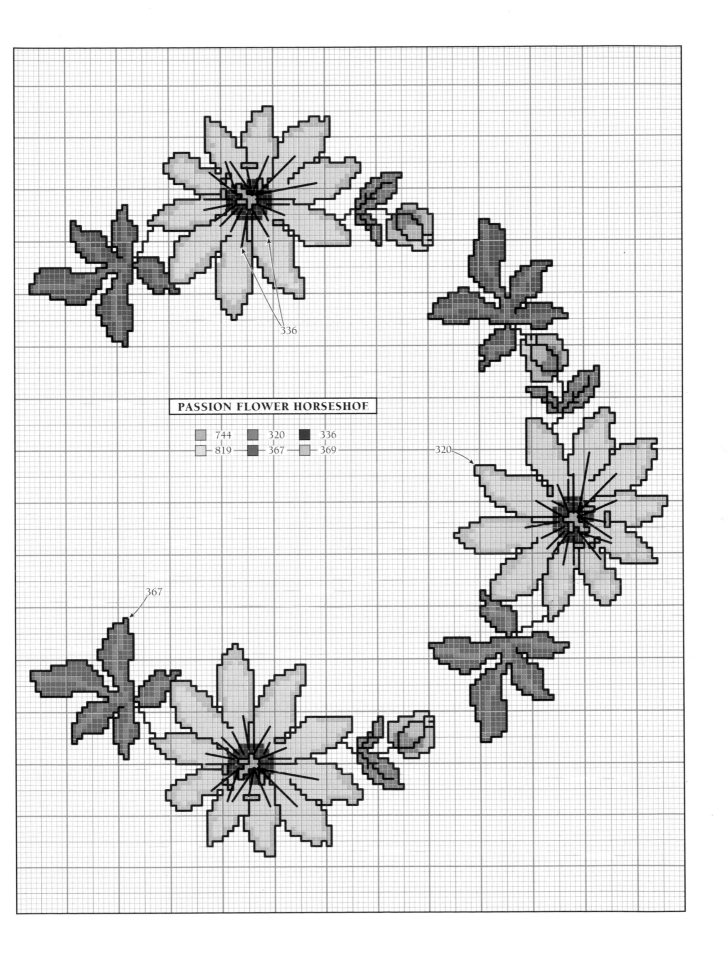

PASSION FLOWER HORSESHOE

| | 744 | | 320 | | 336 |
| | 819 | | 367 | | 369 |

336

367

320

NEW HOME

This quaint, chocolate-box cottage design may be used for a large picture (opposite) or adapted for the useful little wooden tray (page 85). Either would make a suitable gift for many occasions, particularly moving home or a retirement present.
The picture is stitched on a hand-painted evenweave linen and decorated with simple silk ribbon embroidery using straight stitch, lazy daisy stitch and French knots.

THE PICTURE

This design is partly stitched before you paint the fabric. Follow the stitching instructions below but leave the wall in the foreground until you have painted the fabric.

SKILL LEVEL 4
STITCH COUNT: 187 × 139
DESIGN SIZE: 11½ × 8¾ in (29 × 22 cm)

~

MATERIALS
13¾ × 16½ in (35 × 42 cm) Jobelan fabric
(Article 862, shade 223), 32 threads to 1 in (2.5 cm)
Stranded cottons (floss) as listed on the chart
Tapestry needle size 26
One pack each narrow YL 1 silk ribbon in shades,
pink 91, blue 99, blue 117, green 33, green 171
Gouache water-based paints in browns and greens
A stencil brush
Sharp or beading needle
A purchased frame

1. Fold the fabric in four, press lightly and mark the folds with a line of tacking (basting) stitches.

2. Starting in the middle and to the left of a vertical thread, work the cross stitch from the chart on pages 86 and 87, using two strands of stranded cotton (floss) for the cross stitch and one strand for

the backstitch outline. Stitch the oval and its contents, the text, the black cat and the gate. Finally, add the stamens to the border flowers using a long stitch and one strand of stranded cotton (floss) as shown on the chart.

3. Press the stitching on the wrong side (see page 127) to remove all the creases and lay right side up on a clean, flat surface.

4. Mix the water-colour paints or gouache to achieve the shades you want. Using the paint very sparingly, practise on a sheet of paper using the stiff stencil brush in a stippling motion. When you are sure of the technique and colour, stipple the fabric, using greens in the cottage garden and browns or honeys either side of the gate. Stitching detail will be added on top of the painted fabric so do not overdo it!

5. When the cross stitch is complete, refer to the instructions and diagrams below and add the silk ribbon embroidery as shown on the chart. The silk ribbon stitches may be added by eye and at random and so do not need to be counted.

A detail from the New Home Picture showing the simple silk ribbon embroidery, using three basic stitches – straight stitch, lazy daisy stitch and French knots.

6. When the design is complete, stretch and frame as desired (see page 126).

SILK RIBBON EMBROIDERY TECHNIQUES

- Use short lengths (12 in/30 cm) to prevent wearing the ribbon.
- Cut the ribbon at an angle to prevent fraying.
- Knot the end of the ribbon to start, then stitch the loose end to the back of the stitch, using one strand of stranded cotton (floss), snipping the knot off when secure.
- It is probably best to work without a frame, adjusting the stitch tension to suit the design. The tighter the tension, the smaller the stitches.

WILD FLOWER COTTAGE TRAY

I have used a readily available Framecraft tray for this pretty cottage but the atmospheric design would also make a lovely card, suitable for different greetings or messages.

SKILL LEVEL 1
STITCH COUNT: 105 × 60
DESIGN SIZE: 7½ × 4½ in (19 × 11 cm)

~

MATERIALS
11½ × 8¼ in (29 × 21 cm) Yorkshire Aida,
14 blocks to 1 in (2.5 cm)
Stranded cottons (floss) as listed on the chart
Tapestry needle size 24
A purchased wooden tray (see Suppliers, page 133)

1. Fold the fabric in four, press lightly and mark the folds with a line of tacking (basting) stitches.

2. Following the chart on pages 86 and 87, and starting in the middle, work the cross stitch using two strands of stranded cotton (floss) for the cross stitch and one strand for the backstitch outline.

3. When the design is complete, stretch and frame as described by the manufacturers.

~

A traditional cottage worked
to fit a tray or card and embroidered with
an appropriate message makes a lovely
gift for many occasions.

CELEBRATIONS THROUGH THE YEAR

*This section features over twenty fun projects to add sparkle to special dates
in the year, such as Valentine's Day, Mother's and Father's Day, Hallowe'en, Fireworks Night
and, of course, the traditional festivals of Easter and Christmas.
Whether you choose to stitch a plump pumpkin cushion or a fireworks
table centre for those special autumn festivities, or a roomy tote bag for collecting
Easter eggs on a spring day, or a Santa's Sack for storing brightly-wrapped
Christmas presents in the depths of winter, you are sure to enjoy stitching
each and every one of these designs the whole year through.*

~

*These decorative bottle labels make an unusual gift for
Valentine's Day. The Christmas Afghan and cushions pictured opposite will
brighten your home during the Yuletide season.*

HOLLY PLACE SETTING

This bright red tray cloth or place setting to enhance your Christmas table is decorated with a cheerful holly motif. Double hemstitch (nun's stitch) worked in Christmas green and trimmed to the stitching adds a classic edging to this festive project. If preferred, the edge may be hemmed and then frayed to leave a fringe.

SKILL LEVEL 3
STITCH COUNT: Holly motif only 54 × 63
DESIGN SIZE: (including decorative hemstitch)
13 × 20 in (33 × 51 cm)

~

MATERIALS
17 × 24 in (43 × 61 cm) Jobelan fabric
(Article 429, shade 82), 28 threads to 1 in (2.5 cm)
Stranded cottons (floss) as listed on the chart
Tapestry needle size 26

1. Fold the fabric in four, press lightly and mark the folds with a line of tacking (basting) stitches, beginning to the left of a vertical thread (see Where and How to Start, page 12).

2. Position the holly motif centre left of the fabric, at least 2½ in (6 cm) from the raw edge. Following the chart on page 96 and using two strands of stranded cotton (floss) for the cross stitch and one strand for the backstitch outline, work the motif.

continued overleaf

~

*A bumper collection of
ideas to bring Christmas spirit
to your home. Pictured here are
the Christmas Candle Curtains; Christmas
Bauble Apron; Holly Place Setting;
and Christmas Coasters.*

2. Using graph paper and pencil, draw the outline of the letters you need for the name from the Snow-Capped Alphabet chart on page 125 (see Planning Layout Charts, page 8). Arrange these on your master sheet until you are satisfied with the appearance. Add as many holly leaves as you wish and, when you are satisfied with the design, centre the chart and you are ready to stitch.

3. Starting to the left of a vertical thread, work the cross stitch from your chart using three strands of stranded cotton (floss) for the cross stitch. Add any backstitch outline using two strands of stranded cotton (floss) in the shade indicated on the chart.

4. When complete, press lightly on the wrong side and make up as described on page 130.

SANTA'S SACK

This merry Christmas novelty will delight a child of any age, especially if filled with brightly-wrapped festive surprises!

SKILL LEVEL 3
STITCH COUNT: 71 × 97
DESIGN SIZE: 7 × 9½ in (18 × 24 cm)
~
MATERIALS
13 × 30 in (33 × 76 cm) unbleached linen,
20 threads to 1 in (2.5 cm)
Stranded cottons (floss) as listed on the chart
Madeira metallic thread, gold shade 22
1 yd (1 m) tartan or Christmas ribbon for the
drawstring top

1. Fold the fabric in two and press lightly. The design is stitched on one half, the other half is reserved for the back of the sack. Measure 2 in (5 cm) from the fold and mark this point first with a pin, then with a line of tacking (basting) stitches. The snow-capped text will rest on this line. Set aside while you plan the design.

2. Using graph paper and pencil, draw the outline of the fir tree and the Santa's Sack text (see Planning Layout Charts, page 8). When you are satisfied with the design, centre the text and you are ready to stitch.

3. Starting at the left of a vertical thread, work the cross stitch text from your chart, using three strands of stranded cotton (floss). Stitch the fir tree motif, adding cross stitch flames to the tree candles in gold thread as I have done, if you desire.

4. When complete, press lightly on the wrong side and make up as described on pages 129–130.

~

Opposite: *The Snow-capped Alphabet Sampler
and Santa's Sack.*

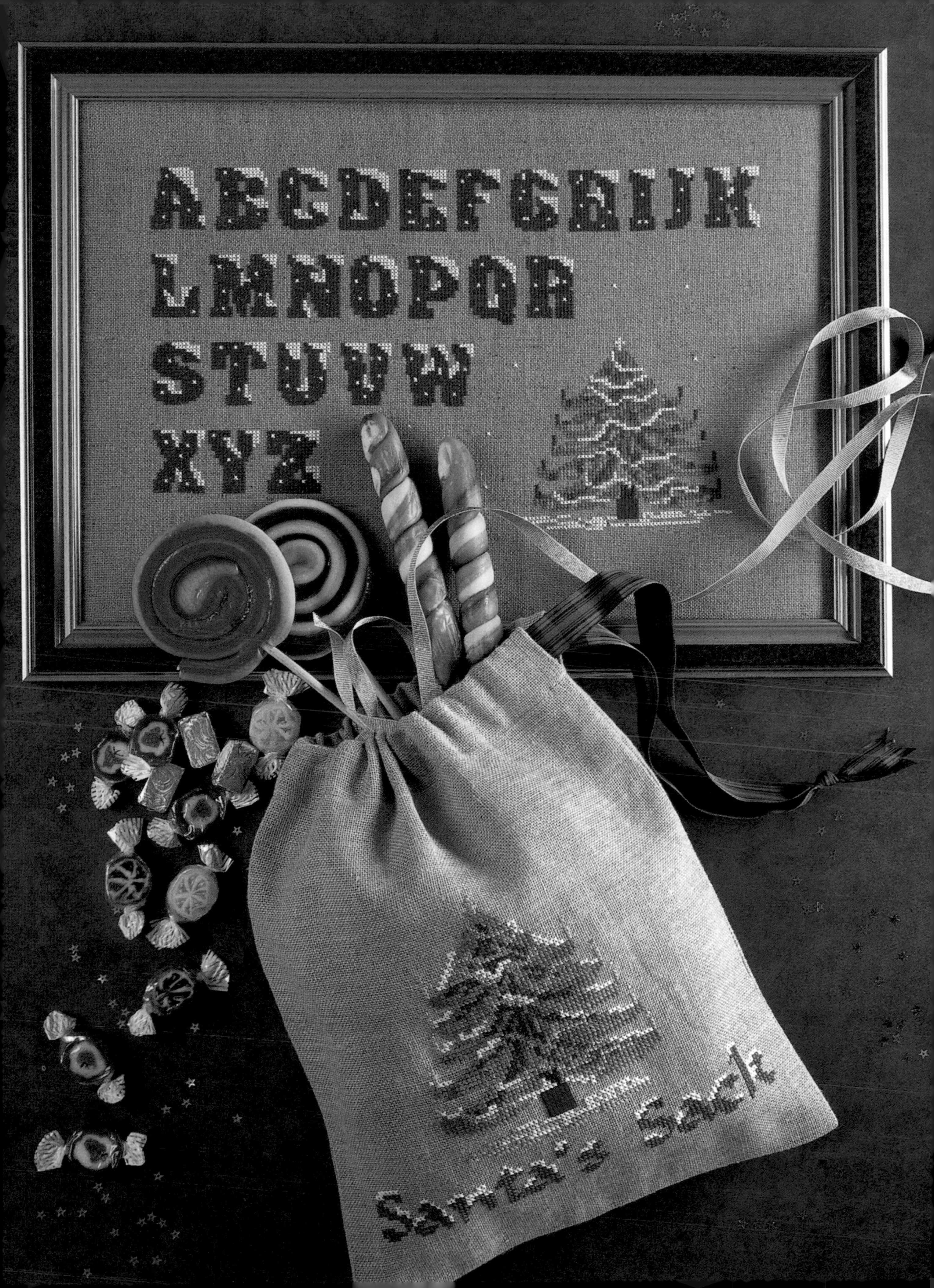
ABCDEFGHIJK
LMNOPQR
STUVW
XYZ
Santa's Sack

EASTER GIFTS

The chicken and egg Easter theme is used to striking effect in the following three projects. The Happy Easter Card is simplicity itself to stitch, while the Easter Surprise Tote bag and Easter Egg Pocket Cushion are more unusual and great fun to make.

HAPPY EASTER CARD

This sweetly simple card is quick to work and made more special by the addition of a two-colour satin bow once mounted.

SKILL LEVEL 1
STITCH COUNT: 72 × 28
DESIGN SIZE: 5¼ × 2¼ in (13 × 5.75 cm)

MATERIALS
6 × 8 in (15 × 20 cm) Yorkshire Aida,
14 blocks to 1 in (2.5 cm)
Stranded cottons (floss) as listed on the chart
Graph paper and pencil
Three-fold card with opening 3¾ × 5½ in (9.5 × 14 cm)
20 in (51 cm) lengths blue and yellow satin ribbon to trim

1. Fold the fabric in four, press lightly and mark the folds with tacking (basting) stitches. Set aside while you plan the design.

2. Using graph paper and a pencil, copy the text required from the chart, add the outline of the single chick, then centre your chart and you are ready to stitch.

3. Starting in the centre, work the cross stitch using two strands of stranded cotton (floss), remembering to keep the top stitches facing in the same direction.

4. Check for missed stitches and make up as described on page 127. Add a yellow and blue ribbon bow to the bottom right corner.

EASTER SURPRISE TOTE BAG

This light-hearted project is worked on gorgeous salmon-pink linen in complete cross stitches. It would be such fun full of Easter treats! Worked on Aida, this would be a Skill Level 1 project, suitable for a beginner.

SKILL LEVEL 3
STITCH COUNT: 146 × 51
DESIGN SIZE: (egg and chick motif only)
10¼ × 3¾ in (26 × 9.5 cm)

MATERIALS
16½ × 28 in (42 × 71 cm) salmon-pink linen,
28 threads to 1 in (2.5 cm)
Stranded cotton (floss) as listed on the chart
Tapestry needle size 26
23 in (58.5 cm) length blue spotted ribbon,
1 in (2.5 cm) width

1. Fold the fabric in two and press lightly. The design is stitched on one section, the other half reserved for the back of the tote bag. Measure 3 in (7.5 cm) from the fold and mark this point first with a pin and then with a line of tacking (basting) stitches. The Easter Surprise text will rest on this line of tacking.

2. Starting to the left of a vertical thread, work the cross stitch text from your chart, using two strands of stranded cotton (floss).

3. When complete, press lightly on the wrong side and make up as described on page 130.

MOTHER'S DAY PINCUSHION

This would make a lovely gift for this special day. It could be converted easily to a card if preferred.

SKILL LEVEL 2
STITCH COUNT: 56 × 40
DESIGN SIZE: 2½ × 1¾ in (6.5 × 4.5 cm)

~

MATERIALS

3 × 4 in (7.5 × 10 cm) white Hardanger fabric,
22 blocks to 1 in (2.5 cm)

Stranded cottons (floss) as listed on the chart

3 × 4 in (7.5 × 10 cm) backing fabric

Stranded cottons (floss) in co-ordinating colours
for the twisted cord

1. Fold the fabric in four, press lightly and mark the folds with a line of tacking (basting) stitches.

2. Following the chart and working from the centre, use one strand of stranded cotton (floss) for the cross stitch and one strand for the backstitch outline.

3. When the cross stitch is complete, check for missed stitches, press on the wrong side and make up as described on page 129.

~

Opposite: **This delicate pincushion makes a lovely gift for mum, while the pencil box is an ideal present for dad.**

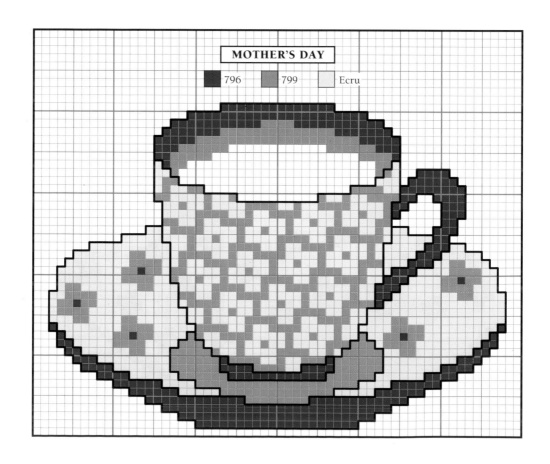

MOTHER'S DAY		
796	799	Ecru

$\mathcal{F}$IREWORK
TABLE CENTRE

An unusual centrepiece for any family party or celebration – the design is stitched in cross stitch on a rich blue Jobelan fabric, using metallic threads and blending filaments to add a sparkle to the stitching.

SKILL LEVEL 3
STITCH COUNT: 295 × 136
DESIGN SIZE: 21 × 9¾ in (53.5 × 25 cm)

~

MATERIALS
14¾ × 26 in (37.5 × 66 cm) Jobelan fabric
(Article 429, shade 61),
28 threads to 1 in (2.5 cm)

Stranded cottons (floss) and metallic
threads as listed on the chart

Tapestry needle size 26

39½ in (1m) bright red or green satin bias binding

16 × 31 in (40.5 × 79 cm) dark blue linen
union for the backing

1. Fold the fabric in four, press lightly and mark the folds with a line of tacking (basting) stitches.

2. Following the chart on pages 122–123 and working from the centre, use two strands of stranded cotton (floss) mixed with blending filaments as indicated on the chart.

3. When complete, check for missed stitches, press on the wrong side and make up as follows.

4. Trim the excess fabric to the desired size, shaping the raw edges as illustrated in the colour picture. Using the shaped stitching as a template, cut the back section in linen union. Place the cross stitch on top of the backing fabric, wrong sides together, matching raw edges. Then attach the satin bias binding as described on page 127.

$\mathcal{M}$AKING UP AND FINISHING TECHNIQUES

This is an important section of the book. You have successfully completed the stitchery – now you must show it off to best advantage. The techniques here show you how.

Many of the designs in this book have been created so that they may be used in the home in a variety of ways, not only as framed pictures, but as cards, cushions and pincushions.

STRETCHING AND MOUNTING

When mounting small cards or novelty projects, the whole procedure can be completed using double-sided adhesive tape, but it is worth taking more time and effort on larger projects. You will need either acid-free mounting board, lightweight foam board or possibly a piece of board covered with a natural fabric such as 100 per cent cotton, which can be fixed in place with a rubber-based adhesive and left to dry.

There are three methods of attaching the needlework to the board before framing.
1. Pin the work to the edge of the board and stick in place with double-sided adhesive tape.
2. Pin to a covered board and stitch in position.
3. Pin to the board and lace across the back with strong linen thread.

When you pin the material to the board it must be centred and stretched evenly, because any wobbles will show when the design is framed. Measure the board across the bottom edge and mark the centre with a pin. Match this to the centre of the bottom edge of the embroidery and, working outwards from the centre, pin through the fabric following a line of threads until all four sides are

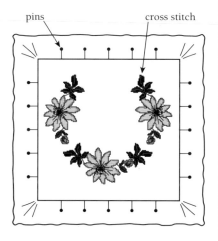

pins   cross stitch

Fig 29 Pinning out the embroidery

stitching method

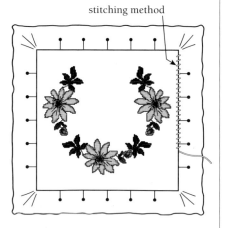

Fig 30 The stitching method

complete. Either stitch through the needlework to the covered board and lace the excess material across the back, or fix with double-sided adhesive tape.

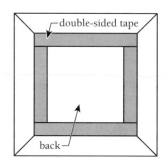

double-sided tape

back

Fig 31 The taping method

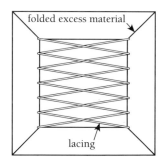

folded excess material

lacing

Fig 32 The lacing method

FRAMES AND MOUNTS

You will see from some of the wonderful colour photographs in the earlier sections of this book that the way in which a design is framed can greatly affect the end appearance. Framing by a professional can be very expensive, particularly if you want something a little different, but most of the framing and finishing techniques suggested here can be tackled by the amateur at home, and this will save a lot of money.

When choosing a frame for a particular project, select the largest moulding you can afford and do not worry if the colour is not suitable. Select a slip as well. This is an additional piece of moulding cut to fit the frame, usually added to give depth and dimension to a frame. Ask the framer to prepare the frame and a coloured or gold slip for you, but buy the frame and glass in kit form (most framers do not mind!) and then decorate the frame yourself.

Adding a mount (mat) can add dimension to very simple projects, as you can see from the colour picture of the Christening Sampler on page 41. You could even try spray-painting the mount to co-ordinate with the frame!

PAINTING FRAMES AND MOUNTS

I use readily available products, for example car spray paint (buy from car repair or body shop suppliers). There are hundreds of colours in the range, but if you have no luck, try bicycle paints which include even more colours! For subtle, matt shades, explore the endless possibilities of emulsion paints from DIY shops, which are often available in tiny tester sizes and are ideal for trial and error.

Before you begin to paint a piece of moulding, take care to cover all nearby surfaces with paper or dust cloths as spray paint goes everywhere! If the moulding is completely untreated, rub down gently with fine sandpaper, clean with white spirit and a soft cloth and allow to dry completely.

If using spray paint, use in a well-ventilated room. Try the spray on waste paper first to perfect the technique. It is better to add a number of light coats rather than one thick layer. Experiment until you find a colour or combination of colours which suit the stitching. Allow to dry completely.

When the paint is dry, you may wish to add a 'distressed' look to the frame. This can be achieved by rubbing the moulding with sandpaper to reveal bare wood or adding polishes to the grooves in the frame. Great effects can be achieved by using contrasting coloured polishes, liming wax, acrylic paints or matt varnish. When you are satisfied with the effect, it is time to assemble the complete project.

ASSEMBLING FRAMES

Ensure that the stitching is stretched and mounted properly (see page 126). Place the frame, face down on a covered surface, and after carefully cleaning both sides of the glass, place in the frame rebate and insert the gold slip. (I add a gold slip to prevent the glass coming into contact with the stitching.) Add the mounted project and backing board, and tape in position.

USING CARDS

There are many blank cards available from needlecraft shops which are simple to make up into a lovely gift. The finishing techniques for cards will vary but the following method should suit most brands.

When the stitching is complete, carefully press the design on the wrong side and set aside. Open the folded card completely and check that the design fits in the opening. Apply a thin coat of adhesive (like UHU) or double-sided adhesive tape, to the inside of the opening (see fig 33).

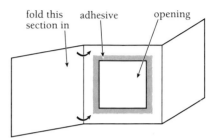

Fig 33 Making up a card

Add the design, carefully checking the position of the stitching and press down firmly. Fold the spare flap inside and stick in place with either double-sided tape or another thin application of adhesive. Leave to dry before closing. Add ribbon trims as desired.

USING BIAS BINDING

Some of the projects in this book are completed using bias binding, which can be either purchased or home-made.

To make bias binding, you will need to cut strips of fabric 1½ in (4 cm) wide across the grain of the fabric and join them as necessary.

To attach bias binding simply and quickly, by hand or machine, proceed as follows. Cut the binding to the correct length. Pin it to the wrong side of the project first, matching raw edges, then machine stitch. Fold the binding to the right side and top stitch into position, then press lightly.

INDEX